Risotto

Risotto

Judith Barrett &
Norma Wasserman

Illustrations by Norma Wasserman

COLLIER BOOKS

Macmillan Publishing Company   New York

Collier Macmillan Publishers   London

Also available in hardcover from Charles Scribner's Sons,
Macmillan Publishing Company

Collier Books
Macmillan Publishing Company
866 Third Avenue, New York, NY 10022
Collier Macmillan Canada, Inc.

Library of Congress Cataloging-in-Publication Data
Barrett, Judith.
Risotto.
Includes index.
1. Cookery (Rice)   2. Cookery, Italian.   I. Wasserman,
Norma.   II. Title.
TX809.R5B365   1989   641.6'318   88-34164
ISBN 0-02-030395-5

Macmillan books are available at special discounts for bulk purchases for
sales promotions, premiums, fund-raising, or educational use.
For details, contact:

Special Sales Director
Macmillan Publishing Company
866 Third Avenue
New York, NY 10022

First Collier Books Edition 1989

10 9

Printed in the United States of America

For
Anne and Rachel
Anna and Tanya

Contents

Acknowledgments

WE are indebted to the meticulous efforts of Pasquale Tatò, language professor and translator—our key to Italian reference materials.

In Milan, Alfio and Rosangela Bocciardia, the gracious owners of the Restaurant Savini, opened their kitchen and shared their knowledge and table with us; Aldo and Pina Bellini of La Scaletta gave us great insights into the *nuova cucina,* new cooking, in Italy.

We also owe our thanks to our agent, Mary Evans, who saw the project through and helped us weather storms along the way. We are grateful to our editors: Maron Waxman, who acquired *Risotto* for Scribners; Rita Rosenkranz, who saw the book go from proposal to finished manuscript; and the others, who helped transform the manuscript into a finished book.

Finally, we want to thank David Barrett for tasting with unflagging enthusiasm almost every risotto we prepared.

Introduction

RISOTTO is the classic rice dish of Northern Italy. Pasta may rule in the rest of Italy but rice reigns in the North, and risotto is its preferred and most popular preparation. You will find it everywhere, from Milan to Venice and from Turin to Como, on restaurant menus and on family dining tables.

In recent years much of the best that Northern Italy has to offer—from food to fashion to furniture—has been welcomed, embraced, and even coveted in America, but risotto is still relatively new here. Many people know of its existence, but few are aware of its place in Italian cuisine, of its dominance over pasta in Northern Italy, or of its special characteristics and versatility.

For years, it seemed to us that risotto was one of those special dishes that you could enjoy only on its native grounds. Thus began our collaboration on this book, which evolved out of a long-standing friendship, a shared professional and personal interest in food, our individual love affairs with risotto as it is prepared in Italy, and our frustration with the unavailability in America of an authentic and convincing version of this delicious and versatile dish.

So two years ago we set out, armed with good appetites and a hefty amount of determination, to discover the "secret" of risotto. We stationed ourselves in Milan, the home of the first recorded risotto, where we sampled five or six different risotto dishes each day. We talked with chefs, restaurateurs, and Milanese women who cook at home.

We returned to our own kitchens to attempt, then to perfect, the method of cooking risotto that we learned in Italy. We used ingredients available in America and familiar measurement standards so that the special tastes of true risotto could be easily duplicated here at home.

The result of our mission is this book, *Risotto*. It includes all of the basic information you will need to cook perfect risotto the first time you try it and every time thereafter. *Risotto* contains over 150 recipes; some are classics, some are recent creations of the *nuova cucina* (new Italian cooking), others are our own. Almost all can be prepared easily and quickly in under 30 minutes.

What Is Risotto?

Risotto is a dish that is simple to prepare, nutritious, economical, versatile and—as you, too, will discover—addictively delicious. It is prepared with a short-grain, highly glutinous rice grown in the Po Valley of Northern Italy. This Italian rice is special in that it absorbs to an unusual degree the flavors of the ingredients with which it is cooked. It also merges with its cooking liquid to create a consistency that the Italians call *all'onda*— "with waves"—while each individual grain of rice remains firm and *al dente*. This combination of full-flavored and still-firm grains of rice, bound with a velvety base, is what gives risotto its unique quality.

No matter what different *condimenti* (flavorings or ingredients) give the risotto its special character, every risotto is created in basically the same way: The *riso* (rice) is first combined with a *soffritto* (a combination of fats and flavorings—usually butter, oil, and minced onion). Simmering *brodo* (broth) is then added to the rice in small increments, allowing the rice to absorb each addition fully before adding the next. When the grains are tender but still firm, there is usually a final addition of broth, butter, and Parmesan cheese, which are stirred vigorously into the rice.

In Italy, risotto, like pasta, is considered a *primo piatto*—the first course of a typical meal that includes several courses brought to the table at carefully paced intervals. Occasionally, risotto is served as an accompaniment to a hearty meat course, most notably with *ossobuco* (braised veal shank).

Although it would be considered unorthodox by Italians, we have found that risotto serves as a satisfying main course at lunch or at dinner. With the simple addition of a salad or vegetable and a crusty loaf of bread, risotto becomes an easy to prepare and elegant meal.

Once you have become familiar with the basic technique, you will discover what a versatile and delicious dish risotto is—whenever you serve it.

Risotto in Italy

No one is sure exactly where the first risotto was created. Because of its similarity to Near Eastern pilaf, some historians say that risotto originated near Venice, a city known as a crossroads for merchants and explorers. Others contend it was a Southern Italian invention.

We do know for certain that the evolution of risotto is integrally tied into the rich history of Italy. The introduction of the rice used in the making of risotto can be traced back to the eleventh century, when Sicily and much of Southern Italy were ruled by the Saracens, Moslems from North Africa. The Saracens' conquests were extensive, reaching as far as the Orient. The short-grained variety of rice used in the making of risotto today was brought to Italy from the Far East.

Where rice was first cultivated in Italy is an historically disputed fact. Some books claim it was in the North, others contend it was near

Naples, the seat of Saracen power. A letter dated September 1475, in which Galeazzo Maria Sforza, Duke of Milan, promised the Duke of Ferrara a gift of twelve sacks of rice for planting, is confirmation that rice growing was firmly established in the Po Valley by that date. The Po Valley, which runs through Piedmont and Lombardy, has climatic conditions—temperature, humidity, and abundance of water—all of which are ideal for rice cultivation.

The legend of the creation of the dish "risotto" dates back to 1574. The story goes that during the 200 years of construction of the Duomo, Milan's fabulous marble-spired cathedral, temporary housing for the workers who came from all parts of Europe was erected behind the church. Among the community of Belgians was Valerius of Flanders, a master glass-worker, who was in charge of executing the stained glass for the cathedral. One of his students had gained a reputation for his color-mixing virtuosity, and rumor had it that he had achieved his brilliant colors by adding a pinch of saffron to his pigments. Valerius taunted him repeatedly, saying, "If you go on like that, you'll end up throwing saffron into your food."

After all the teasing, the young apprentice decided to play a trick on Valerius, choosing the wedding of his master's daughter as his stage. After bribing the cook, a huge mountain of yellow-colored rice appeared for all the guests to eat. Everyone is said to have exclaimed, *"Risus optimus!"* which means in Latin "excellent rice." The yellow rice soon became known as *risotto alla milanese,* and it is still made with a hefty pinch of saffron.

To this day, risotto remains a specialty of the Northern Italian regions of Piedmont, Lombardy, and the three Venezias (Veneto, Trentino–Alto Adige, Friuli–Venezia Giulia). Each of these regions and their towns has evolved its own special preparations for risotto, reflecting both the local foods and traditional cooking styles.

Northern Italy's westernmost region, Piedmont, produces some of Italy's best-known risotti. From Alba, famous for its white truffles, comes *risotto con tartufo bianco,* also known as *risotto alla piemontese.* Piedmont's Barolo, considered Italy's finest wine, is essential for one of its most important risotto dishes, *risotto al Barolo.* The entire hilly area of Piedmont is rich in porcini mushrooms, and here you can find many varieties of mushroom risotti.

Across the Piedmontese border into Lombardy is an even greater array of risotto dishes. Milan, the capital of Lombardy, is the birthplace of Italy's first and most famous risotto, *risotto alla milanese.* Lombardy's extensive production of dairy products is reflected in its risotti, made with the region's local cheeses: Gorgonzola, Taleggio, and Mascarpone. Lombardy's districts of Como, Varese, and Mantua are abundant with small lakes and waterways—the source for the freshwater fish from which many risotti are created.

Farther east in the Veneto region, Padua is noted for its variety of vegetable risotti. From Treviso and Verona, with their fields of radicchio, comes the celebrated *risotto al radicchio.* Seafood risotti abound in Northern Italy's easternmost region. The seacoast in and around the fabled city of Venice is almost synonymous with *risotto nero,* colored and flavored with the ink from squid, as well as *risotto ai frutti di mare,* made with combinations of seafood.

While risotto remains characteristically a Northern Italian dish, it is often found on menus throughout Italy, even as far south as Sicily. Just as the various dialects differ from region to region, so do the preparations for risotto. The basic language, however, always remains the same, and risotto in Italy is always a truly special experience.

Nutrition

There is hardly a family in Northern Italy that doesn't make some variation of risotto often. Risotto is not only good for the palate, it is also good for you.

Rice is a wholesome and nutritious food, without any additives, preservatives, colorings, or other artificial substances. Like pasta, it is composed of carbohydrates, but rice has the added advantage of being more digestible than other complex carbohydrates. Because of the almost total absence of cellulose, rice can be digested in under 2 hours. Most other carbohydrates take 2 to 4 hours to digest.

Rice has just 85 calories in half a cup; it contains the vitamins A, B_1, B_2, and B_6 along with numerous essential minerals, and has merely a trace of sodium. While rice served by itself may lack *all* the elements of a balanced diet, it becomes a complete and even more nutritious food when prepared as risotto, with added fats and protein.

Ancient Japanese monks claimed that a rice diet would renovate the body and spirit in ten days. Risotto, we are convinced, will renew the body and spirit in less than an hour.

Risotto Basics

WE have prepared this chapter as a comprehensive reference source. It will serve to instruct and guide you on all the basic information you will need to prepare perfect risotto.

What struck us most when we ate risotto in Italy was how the creamy consistency of the sauce around the rice was retained from the first bite to the last. The basic technique that we learned, and that is used in this book, will enable you to make risotto with this lasting creamy consistency.

Our instructions differ from the majority of risotto recipes in most other English-language cookbooks in three respects. First we cook the rice for approximately 18 minutes, which is a shorter cooking time—by 5 and even 10 minutes—than most texts recommend.

Second, most of our recipes call for a small quantity of broth to be reserved and added at the very end, when the risotto has finished cooking. It is this last addition of broth, stirred vigorously into the rice, that ensures the creamy consistency of the risotto from the first bite to the last. This step may be omitted when ingredients that already have a high liquid content are added (as noted in the individual recipes).

Third, for diet and health considerations, we have used less butter than is customarily called for in risotto recipes. Instead, it is the last addition of liquid—broth, cream, or particular high moisture cheeses—that makes this possible. You can always add more butter to suit your own taste.

Our basic technique for preparing risotto remains the same for virtually every recipe. And while there are as many variations for risotto as there are condimenti, the basic technique never changes; once you learn it, all of the different recipes will be simple to follow.

Every risotto recipe includes the following:

Brodo, broth, wine, or other cooking liquid, depending on the individual recipe, is the medium used for cooking the rice.

Condimenti—meat, vegetables, seafood, cheese, or whichever ingredient gives the individual risotto its special character—are prepared or readied to be added to the rice. Depending on the recipe, the condimenti can be added at the beginning, in the middle, or at the end of the cooking process.

Soffritto is usually a combination of butter, oil, and finely minced onion sautéed for a few minutes in a heavy pot. The soffritto changes depending on the recipe. Sometimes it has all butter or all oil. The onion is occasionally eliminated altogether or boosted with additional flavorings such as carrot, celery, parsley, garlic, and pancetta.

Riso refers to Arborio rice, which is the main ingredient in all recipes.

Once you become familiar with the basic technique for preparing risotto, you will soon discover that making risotto is not an exact science and that your own cooking sense will serve to guide you. You will quickly develop a feel for the exact amount of liquid you will need, reducing the broth if the condimenti mixture is very liquid or adding water if the broth should run out. You will learn if a little extra butter, Parmesan, parsley, or cream will improve your risotto.

Basic Recipe

This is the basic recipe on which all the variations for risotto in this book are based. It will produce a simple but delicious risotto. For more detailed descriptions of the ingredients called for in this recipe, please refer to the section on the Basic Ingredients that follows.

BRODO	5½ cups Basic Broth, approximately (see Basic Ingredients, page 14), or 5 cups broth and ½ cup dry white wine
SOFFRITTO	2 tablespoons unsalted butter
	1 tablespoon oil (see Basic Ingredients, page 20)
	⅓ cup finely minced onion
RISO	1½ cups Arborio rice (see Basic Ingredients, page 12)
CONDIMENTI	1 tablespoon unsalted butter
	⅓ cup grated Parmesan cheese (see Basic Ingredients, page 19)

1. BRODO: Bring the broth to a steady simmer in a saucepan on top of the stove.

2. SOFFRITTO: Heat the butter and oil in a heavy 4-quart casserole over moderate heat. Add the onion and sauté for 1 to 2 minutes, until it begins to soften, being careful not to brown it.

3. RISO: Add the rice to the soffritto; using a wooden spoon, stir for 1 minute, making sure all the grains are well coated. (If you are using wine, add it now and stir until it is completely absorbed.) Begin to add the simmering broth, ½ cup at a time, stirring frequently. Wait until each addition is almost completely absorbed before adding the next ½ cup, reserving about ¼ cup to add at the end. Stir frequently to prevent sticking.

4. CONDIMENTI: After approximately 18 minutes, when the rice is tender but still firm, add the reserved broth. Turn off the heat and add the condimenti—butter and Parmesan—and stir vigorously to combine with the rice. Serve immediately.

Serves 4

Basic Cooking Tips

Here are some helpful hints to ensure you make perfect risotto every time you cook it.

• *Never* wash the rice! Every bit of Arborio's starch helps make risotto the creamy dish that it is.

• Keep the broth simmering slowly while you add it to the rice. This helps maintain a constant cooking temperature.

• Run your wooden spoon across the bottom of the pot to determine when each addition of broth is almost completely absorbed; you should be able to create a clear wake behind the spoon. The total amount of broth used may vary slightly—within ¼ cup—depending on what other ingredients are added.

• Throughout the cooking process, keep the risotto at an even, lively, but low boil to ensure the proper rate of evaporation of the broth. Since there are approximately 11 additions of broth or liquid within 18 minutes, you can calculate that each addition should be absorbed by the rice in just under 2 minutes. If the heat is too high, the liquid will evaporate too quickly and the rice will stick to the bottom of the pot. If the heat is too low, the broth takes longer to be absorbed, the grains of rice will lose their firmness, and the sauce will not be creamy.

• Taste the risotto frequently toward the end of the cooking process; the total amount of cooking time may vary within 2 to 3 minutes.

• You can add simmering water if you run short on broth.

• Always serve the risotto immediately, for as it cools it will start to lose its velvety consistency.

• Serve risotto in preheated plates.

Timesaving Tips

• Measure out all the ingredients in advance and combine the onion with melted butter and oil in the pot. Have the broth ready to be heated and the ingredients for the condimenti set out and prepared for cooking.

• You can cook risotto in a pressure cooker, a technique described by Franco and Margaret Romagnoli in their book *The New Italian Cooking* (Atlantic/Little, Brown). It takes about half the time, eliminates the frequent stirring called for in the basic technique, and is almost as good as risotto that is prepared in the traditional way. The pressure-cooker method will work for most risotto recipes except those that call for an addition of meat or fish at the beginning of the cooking process. To prepare the risotto in a pressure cooker, follow our basic instructions for the soffritto. Add the rice, wine (if you are using it), and the broth, reserving ¼ cup for the end. Close and seal the cooker's cover, according to manufacturer's instructions, and bring the pressure up to full. Cook for exactly 8 minutes. Immediately bring the pressure down by running the cooker under cold water. Remove the cover, add the final condimenti and reserved broth, and stir vigorously to combine with the rice.

• To simplify the task of cleaning the risotto pot, fill the pot with warm water after you finish serving and allow it to soak while you enjoy your risotto.

Basic Ingredients

RICE (RISO)

Italy is the largest European producer of rice and grows numerous varieties, including some long-grain strains that resemble American long-grain rice. However, it is the short-grain strains, including Arborio, Vialone Nano, and Carnaroli, that are most closely associated with Italian cooking and are best suited for the preparation of risotto. While Vialone Nano and Carnaroli are the first choice for the great restaurateurs in Italy, Arborio rice is the most widely used and available in both Italy and the United States.

If you have ever bought a package of Arborio rice, you may have noticed that the word "Superfino" usually follows the name Arborio. That's because Italian rice varieties are classified according to the size of the individual grains: Comune is the smallest, then there is Semifino, Fino, and Superfino. Superfino denotes the largest grains. All Arborio rice is Superfino.

Long-grain rice, such as American-grown River and Carolina rice, can be used with the risotto recipes in this book, but they will not create a true risotto, with *al dente* grains of rice bound in a velvety sauce. Of the rice varieties available in the United States, only Arborio Superfino rice can absorb the liquid with which it is cooked to such an extraordinary degree and still remain firm.

Arborio rice is widely available in specialty and Italian food stores. If it is not available in your area, you can obtain it by mail from the following sources:

Todaro Brothers Mail Order
557 Second Avenue
New York, NY 10016
212-689-4433

Balducci's Mail Order Dept.
334 East 11th Street
New York, NY 10003
New York State: 1-800-247-2450
National: 1-800-822-1444

Dean & De Luca
Mail Order Service
Suite 304
110 Greene Street
New York, NY 10012
212-431-1691
1-800-221-7714

BROTH (BRODO)

It is important to use a good-quality and flavorful broth, whether it is the kind you prepare yourself from raw ingredients or a ready-made, instant variety.

Although "broth" is technically the term for the cooking liquid that results from the preparation of another dish (for example, a *pot-au-feu* or a *bollito misto*), we are using it as the Italians do. Italian broth is a stock, a flavorful liquid made from meat, chicken, or fish bones and other ingredients.

Meat Broth

In most Italian restaurants, the broth that is used in risotto is a *brodo di carne,* which is usually made with a combination of meat (veal or beef) and chicken.

Since the best stock is always the kind you make yourself, we recommend preparing a large quantity that can be frozen in smaller portions and then defrosted as needed. Our tried and true Basic Broth is made with inexpensive cuts of meat, such as equal parts of veal bones (ribs or shank) and chicken (backs and necks or wings), aromatic flavorings, and cold water to bring out the maximum flavor from the ingredients.

Basic Broth

2 pounds veal bones

2 pounds chicken backs and necks

1 large onion, peeled

4 celery ribs

2 carrots, scraped

3 parsley sprigs

1 tablespoon salt

5½ quarts cold water

1. Place all ingredients in an 8- or 10-quart stockpot and bring to a boil. Skim the foam from the top of the broth.

2. Turn the heat to low and simmer, partially covered, for 2 to 3 hours.

3. Strain the broth into a large container or bowl. Let cool slightly and allow to stand in the refrigerator until cold and the fat has settled on top. Remove fat from the stock with a spoon. Stock is ready to be used. It can be stored for 3 to 4 days in the refrigerator, or can be frozen.

Makes about 16 to 17 cups (enough for 3 risotti)

Chicken Broth

A flavorful chicken broth can also be used in the preparation of risotto with excellent results.

Chicken Broth

3 pounds chicken, whole or parts

2 carrots, scraped

4 celery ribs

1 whole onion, peeled

6 fresh parsley sprigs, washed

1 tablespoon salt

3½ quarts cold water

1. Place all ingredients in an 8- or 10-quart stockpot.

2. Turn the heat to high and bring to a boil. Skim the foam from the top.

3. Turn the heat to low and simmer, partially covered, for 2 hours.

4. Strain the broth into a large container or bowl and allow to cool. Place in the refrigerator for several hours or overnight so that the fat collects on the top. After you spoon the fat from the broth, it is ready to be used.

Makes about 12 cups (enough for 2 risotti)

To use a pressure cooker for either the Meat or Chicken Broth: Place all ingredients listed in the cooker. Add only enough water to fill the cooker two-thirds full. Place top on cooker and follow manufacturer's instructions for using the pressure cooker. Allow broth to cook for 30 minutes for chicken, 45 minutes for meat. Turn off heat and let pressure drop gradually. Proceed with step 4, above.

Instant Broth

In Italian homes, the convenience of a bouillon cube is appreciated as much as it is here. If you want to use instant bouillon, be sure to select the brand you use carefully. Many are overly salty and flavored with seasonings that taste artificial. Almost all have some preservatives in them.

We found that of all the brands in our supermarkets, Knorr bouillon had the best flavor. However, we dilute it with more water than is called for on the package: 1 cube of chicken bouillon combined with 1 cube of beef bouillon and 5 to 6 cups of water. If you use any bouillon cubes in preparing risotto, there is usually no need for additional salt in the recipe.

Canned broth can be an acceptable substitute if it is first simmered for 30 minutes with onion, carrot, and parsley or celery.

Vegetable Broth

For vegetarians, or anyone whose diet does not permit a broth made with meat, vegetable broth can be substituted for the Basic Broth in all of the recipes. As with Basic Broth, you can either make your own or use one of the all-vegetable instant bouillons available in natural-food supermarkets and health-food stores. Since it will be an important flavor of the risotto, be sure you enjoy the flavor of the broth before you use it.

Basic Vegetable Broth

1 large onion, coarsely chopped

1 leek, thoroughly cleaned, coarsely chopped

2 carrots, peeled and coarsely chopped

2 celery ribs, coarsely chopped

2 medium-size turnips, peeled and sliced

3 large tomatoes, cut up

1 small bunch of parsley

1 tablespoon salt

1 teaspoon whole black peppercorns

8 to 10 cups cold water

1. Place all ingredients in a large stockpot and set over high heat. Bring to a boil, cover, and simmer for 1 hour.

2. Strain liquid and it is ready to be used.

Fish Broth

Many of the fish and seafood recipes call for fish broth, which is quick and easy to make because it has to cook for only 20 minutes. Unlike meat broth, which becomes more flavorful the longer you cook it, broth made from fish bones can become bitter if it is cooked too long. To get more flavor into your fish broth remove the fish bones after 20 minutes of cooking, and continue to cook the liquid and aromatic flavorings to concentrate the flavor. Our Basic Fish Broth when added to rice makes a delicious-tasting risotto.

Basic Fish Broth

1 fish frame (scale and head),
    available in fishmarkets (about 2½ pounds)

1 large onion, peeled and sliced

1 carrot, peeled and sliced

1 leek, cleaned, green and white parts sliced

3 parsley sprigs

1 tablespoon salt

1 teaspoon peppercorns

1 cup dry white wine

3 quarts cold water

1. Combine all ingredients in a large stockpot and set over high heat. Bring to a boil, skim the foam from the top, turn heat to low, and simmer for 20 minutes.

2. Strain the liquid and it is ready to be added to risotto.

Makes about 10 cups (enough for 2 risotti)

As with the Basic Broth, a good-quality instant fish bouillon can be substituted for a made-from-scratch fish broth. We recommend doubling the amount of water called for on the bouillon cube package.

If a recipe calls for a particular type of stock (for example, the risotto with shrimp and peas calls for stock made from the shrimp), the recipe for the stock is included with the recipe for the risotto.

WINE (VINO)

There is an Italian saying, *Il riso nasce nell'acqua ed ha da morir nel vino* ("Rice is born in water and must die in wine").

Most recipes in this book call for the option of adding ½ cup of dry white wine to the rice before any broth, at the beginning of the cooking process. The timing ensures that the alcohol evaporates, leaving the essence and flavor of the wine with the risotto. We recommend using one of the less expensive Italian white wines, such as Soave or an Italian Chardonnay. Dry white Vermouth can also be used in place of white wine.

When wine is the principal ingredient of a risotto, as in Risotto al Barolo, Risotto allo Champagne, or Risotto all'Amarone, the method for adding it will vary for each individual recipe.

Wine enhances the flavor of many risotti, but if you prefer not to cook with wine, omit it and add an equal amount of broth in its place.

CHEESE (FORMAGGIO)

Parmesan is the basic cheese called for in most risotto recipes. Although there are many types of Parmesan, Parmigiano-Reggiano is the Parmesan we use when preparing risotto. It has been produced in Italy since Etruscan times, and is today produced under strictly controlled guidelines. Recognizable by the distinctive "Reggiano" imprint on its yellow rind, it is aged as carefully as some valuable wines. Grana Padano, a slightly less aged and less expensive Parmesan, is also a fine choice.

If Parmigiano-Reggiano or Grana is not available, the imported Parmesan you find in jars in supermarkets, which usually comes from Argentina and not Italy, can be used, but cautiously. You may want to decrease the amount, as it lacks the fine flavor of the Italian cheeses and tends to be overly salty. Try to avoid varieties that contain preservatives, since they often have an unpleasant aftertaste.

For the best flavor, we recommend grating the cheese just before, or at least on the same day, you intend to use it. Have it grated at your cheese store, or grate it at home in a food processor or with a hand grater (see Basic Equipment).

If you buy your Parmesan by the piece, and not already grated, it's important to store it carefully so that it will not dry out. We recommend wrapping it first in plastic wrap or foil and then placing it in a tightly sealed plastic container or resealable plastic bag. Whole pieces of the fresh cheese, well wrapped and refrigerated, will keep for weeks, but even when it is stored in the refrigerator, grated Parmesan will begin to lose flavor and dry out after a few days.

Be sure to save your Parmesan rinds. They can be added to soups or stock for a wonderful boost of extra good flavor.

Parmesan can be served at the table, to be sprinkled, when needed, on individual servings of risotto.

BUTTER (BURRO)

All recipes in this book call for unsalted butter. You can use olive oil, vegetable oil, or unsalted margarine as a substitute. However, we don't recommend using salted butter or margarine as they tend to add excess salt to the finished risotto.

CREAM (PANNA)

In place of the final addition of butter, many recipes in this book call for a small addition of cream, which enriches the dish while adding a smoothness to the texture. We generally use light cream. Heavy cream or Mascarpone, the Italian version of crème fraîche, may also be used.

OIL (OLIO)

We like to use olive oil in combination with butter when preparing risotto.

Safflower oil is also widely used in Italian cooking where the flavor of olive oil is not essential to the dish. It can be used in making risotto with excellent results. You can also substitute other vegetable oils, such as corn oil. Stay away from oils such as sesame, peanut, and walnut; their strong flavors will adversely effect the flavor of the risotto.

ONION (CIPOLLA)

All recipes call for yellow onion unless otherwise specified. Shallots or red onion may be used as a substitute. Most recipes call for ⅓ cup chopped onion, which is the equivalent of 1½ ounces or 1 small onion. The onion should be finely minced so that it is barely visible when the risotto is finished.

To chop an onion easily: Peel the onion, cutting away the root end, and cut it lengthwise into halves. Lay the flat sides of the onion halves on the cutting surface and make as many parallel slices as you can, very close together across each onion half. Turn the onion one-quarter turn and make another series of slices at right angles to the first.

PARSLEY (PREZZEMOLO)

Chopped fresh parsley is added to many risotto recipes for color and flavor. Parsley is low in calories, high in vitamins C and A, and rich in potassium, iron, and calcium.

We like to use the flat-leaf parsley, also called Italian parsley, because it has a more intense flavor than the curly-leaf variety. We also find that the flat leaves are easier to chop by hand; curly parsley tends to hop out from under a knife blade.

To chop parsley by hand: Wash and dry the parsley thoroughly. Remove the thickest stems and cluster the leaves together in a small bunch. Using a large chef's knife, cut down on the leaves repeatedly while moving the blade across them. Turn the blade 45 degrees and repeat the action with the knife. Continue to do this until the leaves are chopped fine.

If you use a food processor to chop the parsley: Wash and dry the parsley thoroughly (wet parsley will turn pasty in a food processor). Remove the thickest stems and place the rest of the parsley in the bowl of the food processor. Process until the leaves are chopped fine, about 15 seconds.

SALT AND PEPPER (SALE E PEPE)

When salt and freshly ground pepper are called for in the risotto recipes, it is to flavor the condimenti, not the risotto. Risotto usually will *not* require additional salt and pepper.

Since risotto derives its flavor from the brodo and condimenti, if they are well seasoned, additional salt and pepper should not be necessary.

Basic Equipment

COOKING POT

Most of the recipes in this book should be prepared in a 3½- to 4-quart pot, approximately 8 to 9 inches in diameter, unless you wish to increase or decrease the quantity (see chart that follows) or unless otherwise noted in the recipes. You will have the best results with a heavy enameled cast-iron casserole, such as the type made by Le Creuset or Copco, because, due to their even distribution of heat, the risotto tends to stick less to the bottom of these pots than with other types of pots.

However, in Italy, enameled iron cookware is not readily available and is rarely if ever used. In restaurants, cooks use heavy commercial-gauge aluminum or stainless-steel pots. In Italian homes, stainless steel is the most popular cookware. The important consideration is that the pot be heavy enough so that it will hold the heat evenly.

The larger the quantity of risotto that you prepare, the larger the pot should be, since the cooking time is influenced by the amount of surface area that is exposed to the heat. If a pot is too small, the rice will take too long to cook. If the pot is too large, the stock will boil away before the rice has had a chance to absorb it.

WOODEN SPOON

In the early days, when most cooking was done in copper pans lined with tin or silver, a wooden spoon was essential to protect the pots from becoming scratched and ruined. For risotto, a wooden spoon was doubly necessary because it wouldn't break or harm the individual grains of rice. It is for this second reason that we recommend wooden spoons with long handles always be used when preparing risotto. In addition, wooden spoons won't become hot or melt from the heat of the stove. Besides, they're pleasant to hold and use.

MEASURING CUPS AND SPOONS

You will need a selection of measuring cups. A 2-cup glass measure is the most practical for measuring the rice. You should also have on hand a set of stainless-steel cups that include 1-cup, ½-cup, ⅓-cup, and ¼-cup sizes for portioning out the broth and measuring the condimenti, such as Parmesan and cream. A set of measuring spoons will also come in handy, even though in most recipes precise measurement is not required.

GRATER

We like to grate the Parmesan just before we stir it into the finished risotto; this gives the most flavor. A conventional 4-sided all-purpose kitchen grater is perfectly adequate for grating the small amount of cheese in most recipes. Run the Parmesan along the side with the coarsest grater. You can also grate cheese in a food processor. Turn the processor on and drop small pieces of cheese into the machine while it is running.

There are also special Parmesan cheese graters. While they are actually meant for use at the table, they do get the job done. Another good Parmesan grater is the French Mouli hand grater. It has a rotating grater that works quickly and efficiently.

Many good cheese and specialty food shops will grate fresh Parmesan for you. Only buy as much as you will use in a day or two.

KNIVES

One good 8- or 10-inch chef's knife and a comfortable paring knife are the only cutting implements you'll need. Remember to keep your knives sharp, as this will make any cutting task easier.

Quantity Chart for Basic Risotto

| SERVING | | POT SIZE | RICE | BROTH | SOFFRITTO | | | CONDIMENTI | |
First course	Main course				Butter / Oil		Onion	Parmesan	Butter
2	1	1½ to 2 qt.	¾ c.*	3 c.	1 Tbs.	1 Tbs.	¼ c.	¼ c.	1 Tbs.
4	2	3½ to 4 qt.	1½ c.†	5½ c.†	2 Tbs.†	1 Tbs.†	⅓ c.†	⅓ c.†	1 Tbs.†
6	4	3½ to 4 qt.	2 c.	7 c.	3 Tbs.	1 Tbs.	½ c.	½ c.	2 Tbs.
8	6	6 to 8 qt.	3 c.‡	10½ c.	3 Tbs.	3 Tbs.	¾ c.	¾ c.	3 Tbs.

*For ¾ cup rice, add the broth in ¼-cup increments.
†These are the quantities used in the Basic Recipe.
‡For 3 cups rice, add the broth in ½- to ¾-cup increments.

Classic Risotti

WE created this section of Classic Risotti as a way of introducing you to risotto via "the greats." These eleven risotti are among our favorites. They are also some of the true classics of Italian cuisine, and we wanted to acknowledge them as the great gastronomic achievements that they are.

We had to begin with Risotto alla Milanese, since it is thought to be the first recorded risotto, and has withstood the test of time and trends. Similarly, the risotto with dried porcini mushrooms is an established culinary tradition throughout Italy, from Milan to Sicily. The classics in this section are simple to prepare. The Risotto al Gorgonzola couldn't be easier or better.

Some of the recipes are what we consider to be the new classics. The risotto with strawberries and the risotto with radicchio are examples of the *nuova cucina* (new Italian cooking) and have already become familiar sights on Northern Italian menus. They will surely gain a place in the "Risotto Hall of Fame" one day.

So get to know the Classic Risotti. We come back to these time and again, and you will too.

Saffron

RISOTTO
ALLA MILANESE

For many Milanese today, this risotto remains the most important dish of the city.

Saffron is the key ingredient. Made from the dried stigmas of the *crocus sativus,* it creates an intense yellow color (the word saffron is derived from the Arabic word for "yellow"), and it adds a characteristic but subtle flavor. The best saffron is sold as "threads" in small glass vials. It should be pulverized before it is added to the risotto; otherwise you won't get the bright yellow color or flavor that is characteristic of Risotto alla Milanese. (You can buy saffron that is already powdered, but it tends to be very expensive and is often adulterated.)

Traditional recipes for this risotto call for a spoonful of bone marrow. In Milan today it's not uncommon for even the most traditional restaurants, such as Savini's, to omit the marrow for a lighter taste. Either way, we think the dish is wonderful.

Risotto alla Milanese can be served as a first course, and it is also the traditional accompaniment for *ossobuco,* Braised Veal Shanks (see Index).

BRODO	5 cups Basic Broth (see page 14), approximately
	½ cup dry white wine
SOFFRITTO	3 tablespoons unsalted butter
	⅓ cup finely minced onion
RISO	1½ cups Arborio rice

CONDIMENTI   ¼ teaspoon powdered saffron

1 tablespoon bone marrow (optional, see Note)

1 tablespoon unsalted butter

⅓ cup grated Parmesan cheese

1. BRODO: Bring the broth to a steady simmer in a saucepan on top of the stove.

2. SOFFRITTO: Heat the butter in a heavy 4-quart casserole over moderate heat. Add the onion and sauté for 1 to 2 minutes, until it begins to soften, being careful not to brown it.

3. RISO: Add the rice to the soffritto; using a wooden spoon, stir for 1 minute, making sure all the grains are well coated. Add the wine and stir until it is completely absorbed.

4. CONDIMENTI: Add the saffron (and the bone marrow, if you are using it), and begin to add the simmering broth, ½ cup at a time, stirring frequently. Wait until each addition is almost completely absorbed before adding the next ½ cup, reserving about ¼ cup to add at the end. Stir frequently to prevent sticking.

5. After approximately 18 minutes, when the rice is tender but still firm, add the reserved broth. Turn off the heat and immediately add the remaining condimenti—butter and Parmesan—and stir vigorously to combine with the rice. Serve immediately.

Serves 4

NOTE: Marrow is the fat that accumulates inside bones with age. It is the marrow from the leg bones or shanks of beef animals that is used in this recipe. Traditionally, the bone marrow that is added to the Risotto alla Milanese comes from the braised veal shanks *(ossobuco)*. If you are preparing the two together, simply remove the marrow with a spoon from one or two of the shanks after they have been cooked and add it to the risotto.

To obtain marrow without *ossobuco:* First have your butcher cut some soup bones into 2- or 3-inch pieces; then have the bones split lengthwise into halves. At home wrap the pieces of bone in foil, and place them in a preheated 350°F. oven for 45 minutes. The heat will loosen the marrow from the bones. When the bones are cool enough to handle, scoop out the marrow and proceed with the recipe above.

Dried Porcini Mushrooms

RISOTTO
AI FUNGHI PORCINI SECCHI

Porcini mushrooms, with their full caps and deliciously woodsy flavor, are harvested in Italy in the fall and early spring. They are mushrooms of the *Boletus edulis* species like French cêpes, but porcini (Italian for "piglets") are known for their size. Some grow to as large as 5 pounds or more. When fresh, these mushrooms are firm and flavorful and can be added to a variety of dishes, or they can even be grilled or cooked in butter to create a spectacular main course.

Because the fresh porcini have little in the way of staying power, these mushrooms are traditionally cut and dried at their peak. Don't think you are getting an inferior product when you buy them dried. Dried porcini, which are most often sold in small packets in amounts that vary from about ⅓ to ¾ of an ounce, have an even more intense taste than the fresh mushrooms. While they won't do as a main course, dried porcini can add flavor to soups, omelets, pasta, and risotto. To use dried porcini you have to soak them in hot water. Always add the water in which the mushrooms have soaked to the broth to intensify the porcini flavor.

CONDIMENTI	¾-ounce package dried porcini
	1 tablespoon unsalted butter
	⅓ cup grated Parmesan cheese
	1 tablespoon chopped fresh parsley
BRODO	4 cups Basic Broth (see page 14), approximately
	1 cup porcini liquid, strained
	½ cup dry white wine or broth
SOFFRITTO	2 tablespoons unsalted butter
	1 tablespoon oil
	⅓ cup finely minced onion
RISO	1½ cups Arborio rice

1. CONDIMENTI: Place the dried mushrooms in a small bowl with 1 cup boiling or very hot water. Allow them to stand for 30 minutes. Strain the liquid into a saucepan with the broth and chop the mushrooms coarsely. Set aside.

2. BRODO: Bring the broth, combined with the porcini liquid, to a steady simmer in a saucepan on top of the stove.

3. SOFFRITTO: Heat the butter and oil in a heavy 4-quart casserole over moderate heat. Add the onion and sauté for 1 to 2 minutes, until it begins to soften, being careful not to brown it.

4. RISO: Add the rice to the soffritto; using a wooden spoon, stir for 1 minute, making sure all the grains are well coated. Add the wine and stir until it is completely absorbed. Add the porcini and begin to add the simmering broth, ½ cup at a time, stirring frequently. Wait until each addition is almost completely absorbed before adding the next ½ cup, reserving about ¼ cup to add at the end. Stir frequently to prevent sticking.

5. After approximately 18 minutes, when the rice is tender but still firm, add the reserved broth. Turn off the heat and add the remaining condimenti—butter, Parmesan, and parsley—and stir vigorously to combine with the rice. Serve immediately.

Serves 4

VARIATIONS

1. Marsala wine complements the flavor of the porcini. Add ½ cup dry Marsala in place of the white wine.

2. Add ½ cup fresh or defrosted frozen peas, not cooked, in place of the parsley.

Gorgonzola

RISOTTO
AL GORGONZOLA

Gorgonzola is *the* blue-veined cheese of Italy. Made from cow's milk, it has been produced in the Po Valley since the ninth century A.D. There are several types of Gorgonzola imported from Italy. The strongest and most pungent is *naturale*. The mildest, with a more delicate flavor, is *dolcelatte*. As true Gorgonzola fans, we choose the *naturale* whenever we can find it.

BRODO	5 cups Basic Broth (see page 14), approximately
	½ cup dry white wine or broth
SOFFRITTO	2 tablespoons unsalted butter
	1 tablespoon oil
	⅓ cup finely minced onion
RISO	1½ cups Arborio rice
CONDIMENTI	3 to 4 ounces imported Gorgonzola cheese, rind removed, broken into pieces
	1 tablespoon light cream
	1 tablespoon chopped fresh parsley
	¼ cup grated Parmesan cheese

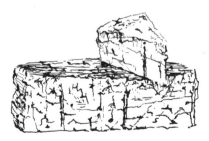

1. BRODO: Bring the broth to a steady simmer in a saucepan on top of the stove.

2. SOFFRITTO: Heat the butter and oil in a heavy 4-quart casserole over moderate heat. Add the onion and sauté for 1 to 2 minutes, until it begins to soften, being careful not to brown it.

3. RISO: Add the rice to the soffritto; using a wooden spoon, stir for 1 minute, making sure all the grains are well coated. Add the wine and stir until it is completely absorbed. Begin to add the simmering broth, ½ cup at a time, stirring frequently. Wait until each addition is almost completely absorbed before adding the next ½ cup, reserving about ¼ cup to add at the end. Stir frequently to prevent sticking.

4. CONDIMENTI: After approximately 18 minutes, when the rice is tender but still firm, add the reserved broth and the condimenti—Gorgonzola, cream, parsley, and Parmesan—and stir vigorously to combine with the rice. Serve immediately.

Serves 4

VARIATION

Top each serving with 1 tablespoon broken walnuts meats.

Spring Vegetables

RISOTTO
ALLA PRIMAVERA

This risotto was first created at Harry's Bar in Venice and has since become established in the national cuisine. *Primavera* is Italian for spring, and this risotto is meant to capture all the best flavors of fresh green spring vegetables. Asparagus tips, tiny peas, and green beans are essential. We like to add some sugar snap peas, diced zucchini, and broccoli flowerets. You can create your own combinations.

The vegetables are simply blanched and added to the finished risotto so they keep their crispness and bright green color. It makes for a dramatic presentation. Some extra Parmesan cheese should be sprinkled on each serving.

CONDIMENTI	2 cups spring vegetables, (asparagus tips, baby peas, green beans, sugar snap peas, broccoli)
	¼ cup light cream
	1 tablespoon chopped fresh parsley
	⅓ cup grated Parmesan cheese
BRODO	5 cups Basic Broth (see page 14), approximately
	½ cup dry white wine or broth
SOFFRITTO	2 tablespoons unsalted butter
	1 tablespoon oil
	⅓ cup finely minced onion
RISO	1½ cups Arborio rice

1. CONDIMENTI: Place the vegetables in a large saucepan and cover with cold water. Place the pan over high heat. When the water comes to a boil, cook for 3 minutes. Immediately drain the vegetables, run them under cold water, and set aside.

2. BRODO: Bring the broth to a steady simmer in a saucepan on top of the stove.

3. SOFFRITTO: Heat the butter and oil in a heavy 4-quart casserole over moderate heat. Add the onion and sauté for 1 to 2 minutes, until it begins to soften, being careful not to brown it.

4. RISO: Add the rice to the soffritto; using a wooden spoon, stir for 1 minute, making sure all the grains are well coated. Add the wine and stir until it is completely absorbed. Begin to add the simmering broth, ½ cup at a time, stirring frequently. Wait until each addition is almost completely absorbed before adding the next ½ cup, reserving about ¼ cup to be added at the end. Stir frequently to prevent sticking.

5. After approximately 18 minutes, when the rice is tender but still firm, add the reserved broth and the condimenti—blanched vegetables, cream, parsley, and Parmesan—and stir vigorously to combine with the rice. Serve immediately.

Serves 4

VARIATIONS

1. Add some whole tender baby carrots or carrots cut into julienne strips to the vegetable mixture.

2. It's not uncommon to be served a Risotto alla Primavera in Italy that is made with a purée of vegetables stirred into the finished risotto. To make a purée of vegetables, follow the directions for blanching. After the water comes to a boil, allow the vegetables to cook for 8 to 10 minutes, or until they are very tender. Drain. Place the vegetables with ¼ cup of the water in which they cooked in a food processor, blender, or food mill, and process until the vegetables reach a smooth consistency. Omit the cream and add to the risotto in step 5 with the condimenti.

Barolo Wine

RISOTTO
AL BAROLO

"King of wine and wine of Kings," as the Piedmontese describe it, Barolo is Italy's finest red wine. Although the best Barolo is well-aged (8 years or more), you can prepare this dish with a younger wine and still produce extraordinary results. There are several methods for preparing this rich, mahogany-colored risotto. We make it in the classic Italian manner by first boiling down the wine to concentrate its full-bodied flavor.

CONDIMENTI	2 cups Barolo wine
	1 tablespoon unsalted butter
	¼ cup grated Parmesan cheese
BRODO	4½ cups Basic Broth (see page 14), approximately
SOFFRITTO	3 tablespoons unsalted butter
	¼ cup finely minced onion
RISO	1½ cups Arborio rice

1. CONDIMENTI: Pour the Barolo into a small saucepan and simmer for about 10 minutes, until it is reduced by half. Set aside.

2. BRODO: Bring the broth to a steady simmer in a saucepan on top of the stove.

3. SOFFRITTO: Heat the butter in a heavy 4-quart casserole over moderate heat. Add the onion and sauté for 1 to 2 minutes, until it begins to soften, being careful not to brown it.

4. *RISO:* Add the rice to the soffritto; using a wooden spoon, stir for 1 minute, making sure all the grains are well coated. Add all but ¼ cup of the Barolo and stir until it is completely absorbed. Begin to add the simmering broth, ½ cup at a time, stirring frequently. Wait until each addition is almost completely absorbed before adding the next ½ cup, reserving about ¼ cup to add at the end. Stir frequently to prevent sticking.

5. After approximately 18 minutes, when the rice is tender but still firm, add the reserved Barolo and broth. Turn off the heat and immediately add the remaining condimenti—butter and Parmesan—and stir vigorously to combine with the rice. Serve immediately.

Serves 4

VARIATIONS

1. For a heartier flavor, add to the soffritto 2 tablespoons finely minced carrot and 1 tablespoon chopped pancetta.

2. Omit the onion in the soffritto.

Chicken, Red & Green Peppers

RISOTTO
ALLA SBIRRAGLIA

Sbirraglia is the name used to describe many variations of risotto that are made with little pieces of chicken. *Sbirri* is the Italian slang word for police force and dates from the nineteenth century when Venice was governed by the Austrians. It is thought that the name implies that the Venetians would have been happy to see the foreign forces cut into small pieces. This recipe is our adaptation of the risotto they make at the restaurant, Harry Cipriani, the New York outpost of the Venice institution, Harry's Bar.

CONDIMENTI	2 tablespoons unsalted butter
	1 boneless chicken breast, approximately ½ pound, skin and cartilage removed, the meat diced
	¼ cup finely chopped green pepper
	¼ cup finely chopped red pepper
	Salt and freshly ground black pepper
	1 tablespoon chopped fresh parsley
	⅓ cup grated Parmesan cheese

BRODO	5 cups Basic Broth (see page 14), approximately
	½ cup dry white wine or broth

SOFFRITTO	2 tablespoons unsalted butter
	1 tablespoon oil
	⅓ cup finely minced onion

RISO	1½ cups Arborio rice

1. CONDIMENTI: Heat the butter in a skillet over moderate heat. When it begins to foam, add the chicken and peppers and sauté for 5 to 10 minutes, until the chicken is cooked through and tender. Add salt and pepper to taste. Turn off heat and set aside.

2. BRODO: Bring the broth to a steady simmer in a saucepan on top of the stove.

3. SOFFRITTO: Heat the butter and oil in a heavy 4-quart casserole over moderate heat. Add the onion and sauté for 1 to 2 minutes, until it begins to soften, being careful not to brown it.

4. RISO: Add the rice to the soffritto; using a wooden spoon, stir for 1 minute, making sure all the grains are well coated. Add the wine and stir until it is completely absorbed. Begin to add the simmering broth, ½ cup at a time, stirring frequently. Wait until each addition is almost completely absorbed before adding the next ½ cup, reserving about ¼ cup to add at the end. Stir frequently to prevent sticking.

5. After approximately 18 minutes, when the rice is tender but still firm, add the reserved broth and the condimenti—the chicken and peppers, parsley, and Parmesan—and stir vigorously to combine with the rice. Serve immediately.

Serves 4

1. To the chicken and peppers, add ⅓-ounce package dried porcini, approximately, which has been soaked in hot water for 30 minutes, well drained and coarsely chopped.

2. Omit the peppers in the soffritto and add 2 ounces chopped pancetta. Add 1 chicken liver, diced, with the chicken breast and 1 tablespoon tomato paste with the first addition of broth.

Spinach

RISOTTO VERDE

This is one of our favorites because it's so versatile. Served as a first course it can precede the lightest or heartiest of entrées. Risotto Verde makes a wonderful main course for lunch, especially when served with roasted red peppers.

CONDIMENTI	10 ounces fresh spinach, or 1 box frozen spinach
	1 tablespoon unsalted butter
	⅓ cup grated Parmesan cheese
BRODO	5½ cups Basic Broth (see page 14), approximately

	3 tablespoons unsalted butter
	⅓ cup finely minced onion
RISO	1½ cups Arborio rice

1. CONDIMENTI: If you are using fresh spinach, remove the stems and wash the leaves thoroughly. Place the wet leaves in a large saucepan over high heat and cook for 3 to 5 minutes, until the leaves are wilted. If you are using frozen spinach, cook according to the directions on the package.

Place the cooked spinach, and ¼ cup of the water in which it was cooked, in a food processor or blender and purée. Set aside.

2. BRODO: Bring the broth to a steady simmer in a saucepan on top of the stove.

3. SOFFRITTO: Heat the butter in a heavy 4-quart casserole over moderate heat. Add the onion and sauté for 1 to 2 minutes, until it begins to soften, being careful not to brown it.

4. RISO: Add the rice to the soffritto; using a wooden spoon, stir for 1 minute, making sure all the grains are well coated. Begin to add the simmering broth, ½ cup at a time, stirring frequently. Wait until each addition is almost completely absorbed before adding the next ½ cup, reserving about ¼ cup to add at the end. Stir frequently to prevent sticking.

5. After approximately 18 minutes, when the rice is tender but still firm, add the reserved broth. Turn off the heat and add the condimenti—spinach purée, butter, and Parmesan—and stir vigorously to combine with the rice. Serve immediately.

Serves 4

VARIATIONS

1. Any portion of spinach can be replaced or supplemented by watercress. Wash the watercress and chop coarsely by hand or in a food processor; add to the finished risotto in step 5.

2. In place of the butter at the end of cooking, add ¼ cup light cream. Risotto Verde is often prepared this way in Italy, and the results are delicious.

3. In Piedmont, Risotto Verde calls for Emmentaler cheese in place of Parmesan. Substitute 3 ounces grated Emmentaler for the Parmesan.

Red Chicory

RISOTTO
AL RADICCHIO

The tender leaves of radicchio may remind you of red cabbage, but the sharp taste will tell you otherwise. Known as "wild chicory," radicchio is native to Northern Italy but is now grown in the United States and is widely available in our stores. The two types of radicchio are the long-stalk variety, called Radicchio Trevisano, and the round-headed Radicchio di Verona.

In Treviso and Verona you'll find radicchio combined with all sorts of other vegetables in risotto, but purists prefer the singular flavor of the radicchio, which mellows with cooking and lends an ever so slight pink hue to the rice.

BRODO	5 cups Basic Broth (see page 14), approximately
	½ cup dry white white or broth
SOFFRITTO	2 tablespoons unsalted butter
	1 tablespoon oil
	⅓ cup finely minced onion
RISO	1½ cups Arborio rice
CONDIMENTI	1 cup finely chopped radicchio leaves
	¼ cup light cream
	1 tablespoon finely chopped fresh parsley
	⅓ cup grated Parmesan cheese

1. BRODO: Bring the broth to a steady simmer in a saucepan on top of the stove.

2. SOFFRITTO: Heat the butter and oil in a heavy 4-quart casserole over moderate heat. Add the onion and sauté for 1 to 2 minutes, until it begins to soften, being careful not to brown it.

3. RISO: Add the rice to the soffritto; using a wooden spoon, stir for 1 minute, making sure all the grains are well coated. Add the wine and stir until it is completely absorbed.

4. CONDIMENTI: Add the radicchio leaves and begin to add the simmering broth, ½ cup at a time, stirring frequently. Wait until each addition is almost completely absorbed before adding the next ½ cup, reserving about ¼ cup to add at the end. Stir frequently to prevent sticking.

5. After approximately 18 minutes, when the rice is tender but still firm, add the reserved broth and the remaining condimenti—cream, parsley, and Parmesan—and stir vigorously to combine with the rice. Serve immediately.

Serves 4

VARIATION

Add 1 cup carrots, cut into 2-inch julienne strips, to the onion and butter mixture before you add the rice. The radicchio blends with the sweet carrots to create harmony for both the palate as well as the eye. This is a beautiful dish to behold.

Strawberries

RISOTTO ALLE FRAGOLE

This is one of the risotti of the *nuova cucina* (new Italian cooking), and a favorite of the young adventurous chefs in Italy. The strawberries produce a surprisingly savory dish; like fruit vinegar, they add a hint of flavor but no sweetness. This is a perfect springtime first course. Follow with grilled salmon steaks and lightly steamed asparagus.

BRODO	5 cups Basic Broth (see page 14), approximately
SOFFRITTO	3 tablespoons unsalted butter
	⅓ cup finely minced onion
	½ cup diced strawberries, washed, hulls and stems removed
	¼ cup sweet Marsala wine
RISO	1½ cups Arborio rice
CONDIMENTI	1 tablespoon unsalted butter
	2 tablespoons grated Parmesan cheese

1. BRODO: Bring the broth to a steady simmer in a saucepan on top of the stove.

2. SOFFRITTO: Heat the butter in a heavy 4-quart casserole over moderate heat. Add the onion and sauté for 1 to 2 minutes, until it begins to soften, being careful not to brown it. Add the strawberries and continue cooking until they begin to loose their red color and give up their juices. Add the Marsala and cook until the liquid in the pot is reduced to about 1 tablespoon.

3. RISO: Add the rice to the soffritto; using a wooden spoon, stir for 1 minute, making sure all the grains are well coated. Begin to add the simmering broth, ½ cup at a time, stirring frequently. Wait until each addition is almost completely absorbed before adding the next ½ cup, reserving about ¼ cup to add at the end. Stir frequently to prevent sticking.

4. CONDIMENTI: After approximately 18 minutes, when the rice is tender but still firm, add the reserved broth and the condimenti— butter and Parmesan—and stir vigorously to combine with the rice. Serve immediately.

Serves 4 to 6

Sun-Dried Tomatoes & Peas

RISOTTO
AI POMODORI SECCHI E PISELLI

Sun-dried tomatoes have been a tradition in Italy for generations. During the dry late summer season, from the North to the South, tomatoes are salted and dried in the open air and preserved for future use. Some dried tomatoes are packed with olive oil; if you buy tomatoes that are simply dried, plump them in oil (see Notes below) before using in cooking. When using sun-dried tomatoes, a light hand is advisable; their flavor is more intense than that of fresh tomatoes and the oil tends to be pungent and salty. The oil in which the tomatoes are stored intensifies the flavor of this risotto.

BRODO	5½ cups Basic Broth (see page 14), approximately
SOFFRITTO	2 tablespoons unsalted butter
	1 tablespoon oil from sun-dried tomatoes
	⅓ cup finely minced onion
RISO	1½ cups Arborio rice
CONDIMENTI	½ cup coarsely chopped sun-dried tomatoes packed in oil
	½ cup fresh peas (about ½ pound unshelled) or defrosted frozen peas, not cooked
	1 tablespoon unsalted butter
	⅓ cup grated Parmesan cheese

1. BRODO: Bring the broth to a steady simmer in a saucepan on top of the stove.

2. SOFFRITTO: Heat the butter and oil in a heavy 4-quart casserole over moderate heat. Add the onion and sauté for 1 to 2 minutes, until it begins to soften, being careful not to brown it.

3. RISO: Add the rice to the soffritto; using a wooden spoon, stir for 1 minute, making sure all the grains are well coated. Begin to add the simmering broth, ½ cup at a time, stirring frequently. Wait until each addition is almost completely absorbed before adding the next ½ cup, reserving about ¼ cup to add at the end. Stir frequently to prevent sticking.

4. CONDIMENTI: After approximately 18 minutes, when the rice is tender but still firm, add the reserved broth and the condimenti—sun-dried tomatoes and peas—and stir well. Turn off the heat and immediately add the butter and Parmesan, and stir vigorously to combine with the rice. Serve immediately.

Serves 4

NOTES: When buying dried tomatoes packed in oil, choose only the reddest tomatoes and avoid inferior, dark brown leathery ones.

If you buy dried tomatoes not packed in oil, they must be "plumped" or reconstituted before you use them. Blanch in boiling water for 1 minute. Drain well and store in a container with virgin olive oil. They can be used the next day.

VARIATION

If fresh and frozen peas are both not available, do not use canned peas. Just omit the peas altogether and substitute 2 tablespoons chopped fresh parsley.

Shrimp, Squid, Mussels, & Clams

RISOTTO
AI FRUTTI DI MARE

This risotto is a Venetian tradition. You can walk into almost any restaurant in Venice and say nothing more than "risotto" and this is what you'll soon find before you. The shrimp, squid, clams, and mussels join forces with the delicately flavored fish broth to produce one of the best risotti we know. The quantities in this recipe have been increased because we find this risotto to be an ideal entrée.

CONDIMENTI   8 Little Neck clams

1 pound mussels, approximately 12

3 tablespoons olive oil

1 large garlic clove, finely minced

1 small tomato, peeled, seeded, and chopped, about ¼ cup

4 ounces medium-size shrimp, approximately 7 to 10 shrimp, shells removed, deveined

4 ounces cleaned squid, including tentacles, cut into 1-inch pieces

¼ cup grated Parmesan cheese

½ cup fresh peas or defrosted frozen peas, not cooked

Salt and freshly ground black pepper

BRODO	5 cups Basic Fish Broth (see page 17), approximately, plus 1 cup broth made from steaming clams and mussels
	½ cup dry white wine

SOFFRITTO	2 tablespoons unsalted butter
	2 tablespoons oil
	½ cup finely minced onion
	1 garlic clove, finely minced

RISO	2 cups Arborio rice

1. CONDIMENTI: Scrub the clams and mussels and place them in a large saucepan with 1 cup water. Cover the pot and bring to a boil. Simmer for about 5 minutes, until the shells open. Discard any shells that do not open. Remove meat from shells and strain liquid through a clean dishtowel or several thicknesses of cheesecloth. Heat the oil in a skillet and add the garlic. Before it starts to brown stir in the tomato, shrimp, and squid, and cook, stirring, for 3 to 5 minutes. Stir in the clams and mussels, add salt and pepper to taste, and set aside.

2. BRODO: Combine the fish broth with the strained liquid from steaming the mussels and clams and bring to a steady simmer in a saucepan on top of the stove.

3. SOFFRITTO: Heat the butter and oil in a heavy 4-quart casserole over moderate heat. Add the onion and garlic and sauté for 1 to 2 minutes, until the onion begins to soften, being careful not to brown it.

4. RISO: Add the rice to the soffritto; using a wooden spoon, stir for 1 minute, making sure all the grains are well coated. Add the wine and stir until it is completely absorbed. Begin to add the simmering broth, ½ cup at a time, stirring frequently. Wait until each addition is almost completely absorbed before adding the next ½ cup, reserving about ¼ cup to add at the end. Stir frequently to prevent sticking.

5. After approximately 18 minutes, when the rice is tender but still firm, add the reserved broth and the condimenti—the seafood, Parmesan, and peas—and stir vigorously to combine with the rice. Serve immediately.

Serves 4 to 6

VARIATIONS

1. You can tailor this dish to your own taste or to whatever seafood is available at your fishmarket. For example, if clams are not available, omit them and make up the difference with more mussels. If squid is not to your liking, increase the quantity of shrimp or add some bay scallops.

2. Substitute 2 tablespoons chopped fresh parsley for the peas.

Cheese Risotti

THE Italian cheeses, from the creamy-soft and sweet-as-butter Robiola to the aromatic and full-bodied hard Parmigiano-Reggiano, create some of the most delicious risotti that are also the easiest to prepare.

Almost every risotto recipe we have seen, with the notable exception of some of the fish and seafood risotti, calls for the addition of at least one type of cheese, usually Parmesan. However, you will find that a variety of cheeses can be added to many types of risotti for an extra dimension of flavor.

We have devoted this chapter to those risotti that are flavored almost exclusively with cheeses and have little else in the way of embellishments. Each distinctive variety, from pungent Gorgonzola to mellow Fontina, from simple mozzarella to the complex Torta di Mascarpone, lends its own unique taste and characteristics to risotto. Just a few ounces can transform the simple taste of a basic risotto into an intensely creamy and flavorful dish.

Cheese risotti can serve as a first course on almost any menu. To prepare the palate for what is to follow, a delicate main course is best preceded by a subtle cheese risotto such as a Risotto alla Fontina or

Torta; while a hearty main course calls for a robust risotto such as a Risotto al Gorgonzola or Taleggio. Accompanied by a simple green salad or vegetable, a cheese risotto becomes an elegant luncheon or light supper entrée.

We recommend several important guidelines when preparing the risotti al formaggio.

Most importantly, the quality of your risotto directly depends upon the quality of the cheese that you use. A little goes a long way, so whenever possible buy the best.

Try to have the cheese at room temperature before adding it to the risotto. It will melt more quickly into the rice. Take the cheese from the refrigerator when you begin preparing the risotto.

With the exception of Parmesan, Gruyère, and Emmentaler, which are grated, all other cheeses in the recipes are soft or semisoft and should be cut into small pieces before they are added to the risotto. This helps the cheese melt quickly into the velvety sauce around the rice.

Try combinations of the cheeses in this chapter for more complicated flavors as well as other cheeses you particularly like. We are continually experimenting and you should too. Even though most recipes call for Italian cheeses, you can have equally fine results by substituting a cheese of comparable quality. (Substitutions are recommended for individual recipes.)

Parmesan Cheese

RISOTTO
AL PARMIGIANO

Lots of freshly grated authentic Parmigiano-Reggiano gives this risotto a rich and tangy flavor. This is the perfect accompaniment to many meat dishes (see chapter on Meat Risotti). In Italy you'll often find this risotto served before a *bollito misto,* a mixture of boiled meats, from which the broth is used to prepare the risotto.

BRODO	5 cups Basic Broth (see page 14), approximately
	½ cup dry white wine or broth
SOFFRITTO	2 tablespoons unsalted butter
	1 tablespoon oil
	⅓ cup finely minced onion
RISO	1½ cups Arborio rice
CONDIMENTI	1 tablespoon unsalted butter
	¾ cup grated Parmigiano-Reggiano cheese or Grana Parmesan (see page 19)
	1 tablespoon chopped fresh parsley

1. BRODO: Bring the broth to a steady simmer in a saucepan on top of the stove.

2. SOFFRITTO: Heat the butter and oil in a heavy 4-quart casserole over moderate heat. Add the onion and sauté for 1 to 2 minutes, until it begins to soften, being careful not to brown it.

3. RISO: Add the rice to the soffritto; using a wooden spoon, stir for 1 minute, making sure all the grains are well coated. Add the wine and stir until it is completely absorbed. Begin to add the simmering broth, ½ cup at a time, stirring frequently. Wait until each addition is almost completely absorbed before adding the next ½ cup, reserving about ¼ cup to add at the end. Stir frequently to prevent sticking.

4. CONDIMENTI: After approximately 18 minutes, when the rice is tender but still firm, add the reserved broth. Turn off the heat and immediately add the condimenti—butter, Parmesan, and parsley—and stir vigorously to combine with the rice. Serve immediately.

Serves 4

Fontina

RISOTTO
ALLA FONTINA

This risotto depends upon authentic Italian Fontina from the Valle d'Aosta region in Piedmont. Made from the milk of cows that graze on the Alpine slopes, Fontina has a nutty, earthy character with a depth of flavor that its imitators do not share. Serve with a rich and full-bodied Piedmontese red wine, such as Barbaresco.

BRODO	5 cups Basic Broth (see page 14), approximately
	½ cup dry white wine or broth
SOFFRITTO	2 tablespoons unsalted butter
	1 tablespoon oil
	⅓ cup finely minced onion
RISO	1½ cups Arborio rice
CONDIMENTI	4 ounces Fontina cheese, at room temperature, rind removed, cut into small cubes
	1 tablespoon chopped fresh parsley

1. BRODO: Bring the broth to a steady simmer in a saucepan on top of the stove.

2. SOFFRITTO: Heat the butter and oil in a heavy 4-quart casserole over moderate heat. Add the onion and sauté for 1 to 2 minutes, until it begins to soften, being careful not to brown it.

3. RISO: Add the rice to the soffritto; using a wooden spoon, stir for 1 minute, making sure all the grains are well coated. Add the wine and stir until completely absorbed. Begin to add the simmering broth, ½ cup at a time, stirring frequently. Wait until each addition is almost completely absorbed before adding the next ½ cup, reserving about ¼ cup to add at the end. Stir frequently to prevent sticking.

4. CONDIMENTI: After approximately 18 minutes, when the rice is tender but still firm, add the reserved broth and the condimenti—Fontina and parsley—and stir vigorously until the cheese is melted and combined with the rice. Serve immediately.

Serves 4

VARIATIONS

1. Add 2 tablespoons chopped prosciutto or smoked ham, such as Westphalian or Black Forest, to the soffritto.

2. For a super-rich risotto, which the Italians call "Risotto con la Fonduta," add 1 cup of hot scalded milk in place of the last cup of broth. Turn off the heat and vigorously stir in 2 egg yolks.

Taleggio

RISOTTO
AL TALEGGIO

In the twelfth century the herdsmen of Lombardy would drive their cows south for the winter. The milk produced en route was called *stracca* or "tired milk," and from this came the *stracchino* cheeses, including Taleggio. There's nothing the least bit tired about this dish; the tangy bite of the Taleggio and the pinch of peperoncino combine to make a piquant dish. Since Taleggio exudes so much moisture when it is cooked, we have omitted the customary last ¼ cup of broth in this recipe.

CONDIMENTI	1 tablespoon unsalted butter
	⅔ cup chopped sweet red pepper
	4 ounces Taleggio cheese, rind removed, cut into small pieces
	2 tablespoons chopped fresh parsley
	Pinch of peperoncino (hot red pepper flakes)
BRODO	5 cups Basic Broth (see page 14), approximately
	½ cup dry white wine or broth
SOFFRITTO	2 tablespoons unsalted butter
	1 tablespoon oil
	⅓ cup finely chopped onion
RISO	1½ cups Arborio rice

1. CONDIMENTI: Heat the butter in a small skillet over moderate heat. When it begins to foam, add the sweet red pepper and cook for 4 to 6 minutes, until the red pepper becomes tender. Set aside.

2. BRODO: Bring the broth to a steady simmer in a saucepan on top of the stove.

3. SOFFRITTO: Heat the butter and oil in a heavy 4-quart casserole over moderate heat. Add the onion and sauté for 1 to 2 minutes, until it begins to soften, being careful not to brown it.

4. RISO: Add the rice to the soffritto; using a wooden spoon, stir for 1 minute, making sure all the grains are well coated. Add the wine and stir until it is completely absorbed. Begin to add the simmering broth, ½ cup at a time, stirring frequently. Wait until each addition is almost completely absorbed before adding the next ½ cup. Stir frequently to prevent sticking.

5. After approximately 18 minutes, when the rice is tender but still firm, add the condimenti—Taleggio, sautéed red pepper, parsley, and peperoncino—and stir vigorously until the cheese is melted and combined with the rice. Serve immediately.

Serves 4

Mascarpone

RISOTTO
AL MASCARPONE

An old Milanese passion, Mascarpone is Italy's version of French *crème fraîche* or our own much less refined sour cream. It is essentially solidified cream, mildly acidulated and whipped up into a velvety consistency. In risotto it lends a rich and creamy if slightly tangy taste. Originally produced in Lombardy only in the fall and winter months, it is now available all year round. Mascarpone is usually sold in small 100-gram containers in specialty cheese shops and some supermarkets.

BRODO   5 cups Basic Broth (see page 14), approximately

½ cup dry white wine or broth

SOFFRITTO	2 tablespoons unsalted butter
	1 tablespoon oil
	⅓ cup finely minced onion
RISO	1½ cups Arborio rice
CONDIMENTI	⅓ cup Mascarpone cheese (100-gram container)
	¼ cup grated Parmesan cheese
	1 tablespoon chopped fresh parsley

1. BRODO: Bring the broth to a steady simmer in a saucepan on top of the stove.

2. SOFFRITTO: Heat the butter and oil in a heavy 4-quart casserole over moderate heat. Add the onion and sauté for 1 to 2 minutes, until it begins to soften, being careful not to brown it.

3. RISO: Add the rice to the soffritto; using a wooden spoon, stir for 1 minute, making sure all the grains are well coated. Add the wine and stir until it is almost completely absorbed. Begin to add the simmering broth, ½ cup at a time, stirring frequently. Wait until each addition is almost completely absorbed before adding the next ½ cup, reserving about ¼ cup to add at the end. Stir frequently to prevent sticking.

4. CONDIMENTI: After approximately 18 minutes, when the rice is tender but still firm, add the reserved broth and the condimenti—Mascarpone, Parmesan, and parsley—and stir vigorously until the cheeses are melted and combined with the rice. Serve immediately.

Serves 4

VARIATION

Add ⅓ cup fresh strawberries or seedless grapes, fineley chopped, after the rice has been cooking for 10 minutes.

Mozzarella

════════

For best results, we like to use fresh mozzarella with its just-made milky taste and soft, tender texture. It produces a light and delicately flavored risotto. Commercially packaged mozzarella makes a heavier-textured but also delicious risotto. The only mozzarella not recommended for risotto is imported Italian *mozzarella di bufala,* made from water buffalo milk. Although it is fresh, when cooked or melted it becomes extremely stringy.

BRODO	5 cups Basic Broth (see page 14), approximately
	½ cup dry white wine or broth
SOFFRITTO	2 tablespoons unsalted butter
	1 tablespoon oil
	⅓ cup finely minced onion
RISO	1½ cups Arborio rice
CONDIMENTI	4 ounces mozzarella cheese, cut into small pieces
	1 tablespoon unsalted butter
	¼ cup grated Parmesan cheese
	1 tablespoon chopped fresh parsley

1. BRODO: Bring the broth to a steady simmer in a saucepan on top of the stove.

2. SOFFRITTO: Heat the butter and oil in a heavy 4-quart casserole over moderate heat. Add the onion and sauté for 1 to 2 minutes, until it begins to soften, being careful not to brown it.

3. RISO: Add the rice to the soffritto; using a wooden spoon, stir for 1 minute, making sure all the grains are well coated. Add the wine and stir until it is completely absorbed. Begin to add the simmering broth, ½ cup at a time, stirring frequently. Wait until each addition is almost completely absorbed before adding the next ½ cup, reserving about ¼ cup to add at the end. Stir frequently to prevent sticking.

4. CONDIMENTI: After approximately 18 minutes, when the rice is tender but still firm, add the reserved broth. Turn off the heat and immediately add the condimenti—mozzarella, butter, Parmesan, and parsley—and stir vigorously until the cheeses are melted and combined with the rice. Serve immediately.

Serves 4

VARIATION

For a robust flavor, use smoked mozzarella. Remove the rind, cut into small pieces, and substitute ¼ cup Mascarpone for the butter in step 4.

Ricotta

RISOTTO
ALLA RICOTTA

Fresh ricotta, with its soft curds and mild taste, makes this risotto with spinach extremely creamy. Another good choice, if you can find it, is imported Italian ricotta, which is denser and richer than American-made ricottas. If you use the imported variety, add a full cup and omit the spinach. Do not confuse the imported fresh ricotta with imported Ricotta Pecorino, which is a mildly pungent table or eating cheese made from sheep's milk. It is not recommended for this recipe.

BRODO	5 cups Basic Broth (see page 14), approximately
	½ cup dry white wine or broth
SOFFRITTO	2 tablespoons unsalted butter
	1 tablespoon oil
	⅓ cup finely minced onion
RISO	1½ cups Arborio rice
CONDIMENTI	½ cup whole-milk ricotta cheese
	½ cup finely chopped fresh spinach leaves, washed and stems removed
	¼ cup grated Parmesan cheese

1. BRODO: Bring the broth to a steady simmer in a saucepan on top of the stove.

2. *SOFFRITTO:* Heat the butter and oil in a heavy 4-quart casserole over moderate heat. Add the onion and sauté for 1 to 2 minutes, until it begins to soften, being careful not to brown it.

3. *RISO:* Add the rice to the soffritto; using a wooden spoon, stir for 1 minute, making sure all the grains are well coated. Add the wine and stir until it is almost completely absorbed. Begin to add the simmering broth, ½ cup at a time, stirring frequently. Wait until each addition is almost completely absorbed before adding the next ½ cup, reserving about ¼ cup to add at the end. Stir frequently to prevent sticking.

4. *CONDIMENTI:* After approximately 18 minutes, when the rice is tender but still firm, add the reserved broth and the condimenti—ricotta, spinach, and Parmesan—and stir vigorously to combine with the rice. Serve immediately.

Serves 4

Four Cheeses

RISOTTO
AI QUATTRO FORMAGGI

This is our adaptation of the classic pasta sauce. You can choose the cheeses to your own taste. We are partial to the combination of Fontina, Gorgonzola, Taleggio, and Parmesan for a rich complexity of flavors. For best results, remember to have the cheeses at room temperature.

BRODO	5 cups Basic Broth (see page 14), approximately
	½ cup dry white wine or broth
SOFFRITTO	2 tablespoons unsalted butter
	1 tablespoon oil
	⅓ cup finely minced onion
RISO	1½ cups Arborio rice
CONDIMENTI	1 to 2 ounces Gorgonzola cheese, cut into cubes (see Variations)
	1 to 2 ounces Fontina cheese, rind removed, cut into cubes
	1 to 2 ounces Taleggio cheese, rind removed, cut into cubes
	¼ cup grated Parmesan cheese
	1 tablespoon chopped fresh parsley

1. BRODO: Bring the broth to a steady simmer in a saucepan on top of the stove.

2. SOFFRITTO: Heat the butter and oil in a heavy 4-quart casserole over moderate heat. Add the onion and sauté for 1 to 2 minutes, until it begins to soften, being careful not to brown it.

3. RISO: Add the rice to the soffritto; using a wooden spoon, stir for 1 minute, making sure all the grains are well coated. Add the wine and stir until it is almost completely absorbed. Begin to add the simmering broth, ½ cup at a time, stirring frequently. Wait until each addition is almost completely absorbed before adding the next ½ cup, reserving about ¼ cup to add at the end. Stir frequently to prevent sticking.

4. CONDIMENTI: After approximately 18 minutes, when the rice is tender but still firm, add the reserved broth and the condimenti—

Gorgonzola, Fontina, Taleggio, Parmesan, and parsley—and stir vigorously until the cheeses are melted and combined with the rice. Serve immediately.

Serves 4

1. Any good-quality blue cheese such as Roquefort, Blue Castello, or Saga Blue can be used in place of the Gorgonzola.

2. If the combination of cheeses proves too strong for your taste, reduce the amount of Gorgonzola and substitute 2 ounces mozzarella.

Gruyère

RISOTTO
ALLA GROVIERA

In Piedmont, the northernmost province of Italy abutting Switzerland, we tasted risotto prepared with the classic Swiss cheese, Gruyère. Even though the Italians produce their version of Gruyère called *Groviera,* it is the Gruyère from Switzerland that is most commonly found throughout Italy. In this risotto, it lends its characteristic nutty flavor. Serve as a first course before veal roll stuffed with pancetta and sage.

| BRODO | 5 cups Basic Broth (see page 14), approximately |
| | ½ cup dry white wine or broth |

SOFFRITTO	2 tablespoons unsalted butter
	1 tablespoon oil
	⅓ cup finely minced onion

| RISO | 1½ cups Arborio rice |

CONDIMENTI	4 ounces Gruyère cheese, rind removed, coarsely grated or chopped
	¼ cup grated Parmesan cheese
	2 tablespoons chopped fresh parsley

1. BRODO: Bring the broth to a steady simmer in a saucepan on top of the stove.

2. SOFFRITTO: Heat the butter and oil in a heavy 4-quart casserole over moderate heat. Add the onion and sauté for 1 to 2 minutes, until it begins to soften, being careful not to brown it.

3. RISO: Add the rice to the soffritto; using a wooden spoon, stir for 1 minute, making sure all the grains are well coated. Add the wine and stir until it is almost completely absorbed. Begin to add the simmering broth, ½ cup at a time, stirring frequently. Wait until each addition is almost completely absorbed before adding the next ½ cup, reserving about ¼ cup to add at the end. Stir frequently to prevent sticking.

4. CONDIMENTI: After approximately 18 minutes, when the rice is tender but still firm, add the reserved broth and the condimenti— Gruyère, Parmesan, and parsley—and stir vigorously until the cheeses are melted and combined with the rice. Serve immediately.

Serves 4

VARIATIONS

1. Add 3 tablespoons chopped carrot and 3 tablespoons chopped celery ribs to the soffritto.

2. Eliminate the parsley and add ½ cup chopped fresh spinach with the Gruyère cheese.

Robiola

RISOTTO
ALLA ROBIOLA

This risotto is so delicious that it is surprising to find it so easy to prepare. The Robiola cheeses, which include Annabella and Fruttosella, are creamy, rich, moist, and very fresh cheeses from Lombardy and Piedmont. Like the Tortas (see Index) they are available plain or with a variety of flavorings, such as herbs, fruits, smoked salmon, or green peppercorns. You can use any of the Robiola cheeses in this recipe with wonderful results.

BRODO	5½ cups Basic Broth (see page 14), approximately
SOFFRITTO	2 tablespoons unsalted butter
	1 tablespoon oil
	⅓ cup finely minced onion
RISO	1½ cups Arborio rice
CONDIMENTI	1 package Robiola cheese, approximately 3 ounces

1. BRODO: Bring the broth to a steady simmer in a saucepan on top of the stove.

2. SOFFRITTO: Heat the butter and oil in a heavy 4-quart casserole over moderate heat. Add the onion and sauté for 1 to 2 minutes, until it begins to soften, being careful not to brown it.

3. RISO: Add the rice to the soffritto; using a wooden spoon, stir for 1 minute, making sure all the grains are well coated. Begin to add the simmering broth, ½ cup at a time, stirring frequently. Wait until each addition is almost completely absorbed before adding the next ½ cup, reserving about ¼ cup to add at the end. Stir frequently to prevent sticking.

4. CONDIMENTI: After approximately 18 minutes, when the rice is tender but still firm, add the reserved broth and the condimenti—the Robiola—and stir vigorously until the cheese is melted and combined with the rice. Serve immediately.

Serves 4

Goat Cheese

RISOTTO
AL FORMAGGIO CAPRINO

We are happy to see Formaggio di Capra finally taking its rightful place next to the well-established French chèvres. The Italian *caprini* or goat cheeses tend to be less salty and milder than their Gallic counterparts, and we have found them especially well suited to risotto. For this recipe use only young, fresh goat cheeses without rinds, such as Caprini, Capra Fresca, or Novarigo. These are produced either plain or seasoned with a variety of herbs or flavorings. All yield different but delicious results.

BRODO	5½ cups Basic Broth (see page 14), approximately
SOFFRITTO	2 tablespoons unsalted butter
	1 tablespoon oil
	⅓ cup finely minced onion
RISO	1½ cups Arborio rice
CONDIMENTI	4 ounces goat cheese, cut into small pieces
	1 tablespoon unsalted butter
	¼ cup chopped fresh parsley

1. BRODO: Bring the broth to a steady simmer in a saucepan on top of the stove.
2. SOFFRITTO: Heat the butter and oil in a heavy 4-quart casse-

role over moderate heat. Add the onion and sauté for 1 to 2 minutes, until it begins to soften, being careful not to brown it.

3. *RISO:* Add the rice to the soffritto; using a wooden spoon, stir for 1 minute, making sure all the grains are well coated. Begin to add the simmering broth, ½ cup at a time, stirring frequently. Wait until each addition is almost completely absorbed before adding the next ½ cup, reserving about ¼ cup to add at the end. Stir frequently to prevent sticking.

4. *CONDIMENTI:* After approximately 18 minutes, when the rice is tender but still firm, add the reserved broth and the condimenti—goat cheese, butter, and parsley—and stir vigorously until the cheese is melted and combined with the rice. Serve immediately.

Serves 4

VARIATIONS

1. Good substitutes include the French-made Montrachet or Lingot or the fresh domestic soft goat cheeses.

2. Sauté ¼ cup pine nuts in 1 tablespoon unsalted butter for 3 to 5 minutes, or until they begin to turn golden. Use some as a garnish for each serving.

Camembert

RISOTTO
AL CAMEMBERT

The recent availability of Italian soft-ripened cheeses inspired us to prepare risotto with cheeses from the Brie family, which includes Camembert. The results were splendid; not only does the risotto capture all of the flavor of the cheese, but it creates a satinlike texture. Whether you use French or Italian, any good-quality Brie or Camembert will do as long as it is not overripe. Trim away all of the rind when the cheese is cold and firm. It may appear that you lose a lot of the cheese by cutting off the rind, but there will be enough left for your risotto.

BRODO	5½ cups Basic Broth (see page 14), approximately
SOFFRITTO	3 tablespoons unsalted butter
	⅓ cup finely minced onion
RISO	1½ cups Arborio rice
CONDIMENTI	1 whole Camembert cheese, 7 to 8 ounces, or 8 ounces Brie cheese, rind removed, cut into small pieces

1. BRODO: Bring the broth to a steady simmer in a saucepan on top of the stove.

2. SOFFRITTO: Heat the butter in a heavy 4-quart casserole over moderate heat. Add the onion and sauté for 1 to 2 minutes, until it begins to soften, being careful not to brown it.

3. RISO: Add the rice to the soffritto; using a wooden spoon, stir for 1 minute, making sure all the grains are well coated. Begin to add the simmering broth, ½ cup at a time, stirring frequently to prevent sticking. Wait until each addition is almost completely absorbed before adding the next ½ cup. Stir frequently.

4. CONDIMENTI: After approximately 18 minutes, when the rice is tender but still firm, add the condimenti—Camembert or Brie—and stir vigorously until the cheese is melted and combined with the rice. Serve immediately.

Serves 4

Torta

RISOTTO
ALLA TORTA DI FORMAGGIO

Torta is the Italian word for cake, and it is the perfect description for these cheeses made of alternating layers of Mascarpone cheese with a variety of complementary ingredients. This delicious confection is the invention of Peck's, Milan's premier food emporium, where we counted no fewer than a dozen different Tortas displayed like pastries in a sweet shop. The most common Torta is made with Gorgonzola, but you can find more exotic varieties spiked with such delicacies as *funghi* (mushrooms), *fichi* (figs), *salmone* (smoked salmon), and *basilico* (basil and pine nuts). Risotto made with any of these store-bought Tortas will be extremely rich and wonderfully tasty. Our favorite is made with the Torta al Basilico. It's a special treat in the winter when we miss the fresh taste of summer pesto.

BRODO	5 cups Basic Broth (see page 14), approximately
	½ cup dry white wine

SOFFRITTO	2 tablespoons unsalted butter
	1 tablespoon oil
	⅓ cup finely minced onion

RISO	1½ cups Arborio rice

CONDIMENTI	⅓ pound Torta with basil and pine nuts
	1 tablespoon unsalted butter
	¼ cup grated Parmesan cheese
	1 tablespoon finely minced fresh basil

1. BRODO: Bring the broth to a steady simmer in a saucepan on top of the stove.

2. SOFFRITTO: Heat the butter and oil in a heavy 4-quart casserole over moderate heat. Add the onion and sauté for 1 to 2 minutes, until it begins to soften, being careful not to brown it.

3. RISO: Add the rice to the soffritto; using a wooden spoon, stir

for 1 to 2 minutes, making sure all the grains are well coated. Add the wine and stir until it is completely absorbed. Begin to add the broth, ½ cup at a time. Wait until each addition is almost completely absorbed before adding the next ½ cup. Stir frequently to prevent sticking.

4. CONDIMENTI: After 18 minutes, when the rice is tender but still firm, turn off the heat and immediately add the last ½ cup broth, and the condimenti—the Torta, remaining butter, and Parmesan cheese— and stir vigorously to combine with the rice. Top each serving with chopped fresh basil.

Serves 4

VARIATION

When using another Torta, eliminate the basil and stir in 1 table-spoon finely chopped fresh parsley before serving.

Vegetable Risotti

THE Italian way with vegetables is a study in diversity and simplicity, so it is not surprising that the *risotti alla verdura,* vegetable risotti, are the most numerous and certainly among the easiest to prepare.

It takes very little to make risotto great, and that is clearly apparent in the vast array of vegetable risotti. All you need is a small quantity of chopped spinach, a handful of fresh peas, just two julienned leeks, or a simple carrot to make a colorful and deliciously fresh-tasting risotto.

Almost every vegetable we've come across, whether it's leafy green or hardy and bulbous, is delicious in risotto. In fact, as this chapter grew like Jack's proverbial beanstalk, we began to wonder where we would ever be able to stop.

Because of sheer numbers, we divided this section into three parts. "Strictly Green" risotti are made with green vegetables only and no meat of any sort. These are best served as the first course of a meal. The "Colorful" risotti are more complex, incorporating several vegetables or herbs and occasionally some meat or ham for flavoring; these can be served either as a first course or as a luncheon or light supper entrée. The "Mushroom" risotti, the heartiest in this chapter, include recipes using both fresh mushrooms, wild and cultivated varieties, and dried porcini, a staple of Italian cookery. These can also serve as the main course for lunch or dinner.

When choosing vegetables for risotto, always select the freshest, best-quality produce. The quality of your *risotti alla verdura* will depend upon the quality of the vegetables.

Strict vegetarians can replace the Basic Broth of meat and chicken, called for in all of the recipes, with Basic Vegetable Broth (see Index). In those recipes that call for meat and ham as flavorings, the meat can always be omitted.

We hope that you will follow our lead and use this chapter as a starting point for your own creations.

Strictly Green Risotti

Asparagus

RISOTTO
CON GLI ASPARAGI

Although asparagus arrives at the market earlier each year, and stays longer, the best still comes in the early spring. Select the skinniest spears for this risotto; they're the most tender and impart a delicate "grassy" flavor.

BRODO	5 cups Basic Broth (see page 14), approximately
	½ cup dry white wine or broth
SOFFRITTO	2 tablespoons unsalted butter
	1 tablespoon oil
	⅓ cup finely minced onion
RISO	1½ cups Arborio rice
CONDIMENTI	¾ pound fresh asparagus, washed, cut into 1-inch pieces, tough bottom parts discarded and tips reserved separately
	1 tablespoon unsalted butter
	¼ cup grated Parmesan cheese

1. BRODO: Bring the broth to a steady simmer in a saucepan on top of the stove.

2. SOFFRITTO: Heat the butter and oil in a heavy 4-quart casserole over moderate heat. Add the onion and sauté for 1 to 2 minutes, until it begins to soften, being careful not to brown it.

3. RISO: Add the rice to the soffritto; using a wooden spoon, stir for 1 minute, making sure all the grains are well coated. Add the wine and stir until it is completely absorbed.

4. CONDIMENTI: Add the asparagus, reserving the tips, and begin to add the simmering broth, ½ cup at a time, stirring frequently. Wait until each addition is almost completely absorbed before adding the next ½ cup, reserving about ¼ cup to add at the end. Add the asparagus tips after the rice has been cooking for 10 to 12 minutes and continue to add the broth, ½ cup at a time. Stir frequently to prevent sticking.

5. After approximately 18 minutes, when the rice is tender but still firm, add the reserved broth. Turn off the heat and immediately add the remaining condimenti—butter and Parmesan—and stir vigorously to combine with the rice. Serve immediately.

Serves 4

VARIATIONS

1. In Lombardy, it is not unusual to use the asparagus tips as a garnish to a simple basic risotto. Steam or boil the asparagus tips in water. When the basic risotto is finished cooking, garnish each serving with several asparagus tips.

2. Add ¼ cup of chopped fresh parsley and 1 garlic clove, finely minced, to the soffritto. Continue with the recipe.

3. Omit the butter in the last step and substitute ¼ cup light cream.

Artichoke

RISOTTO
CON I CARCIOFI

This is one of our favorite luncheon risotti to serve in the early spring when artichokes are very fresh. You can prepare this recipe with just one medium-size artichoke or two smaller ones. We discovered the addition of Mascarpone cheese in this risotto at the Restaurant Peck, the elegant eatery housed beneath Milan's most famous food store. Serve this risotto after a first course of fresh figs or melon and thin-sliced prosciutto, and follow it with a salad of chopped arugula and radicchio with just enough extra-virgin olive oil and a hearty wine vinegar to coat the leaves.

CONDIMENTI	1 medium-size artichoke, or 2 small artichokes
	½ lemon
	¼ cup Mascarpone cheese
	¼ cup grated Parmesan cheese
	2 tablespoons chopped fresh parsley

BRODO	5 cups Basic Broth (see page 14), approximately
	½ cup dry white wine or broth

SOFFRITTO	2 tablespoons unsalted butter
	1 tablespoon oil
	⅓ cup finely minced onion
	1 garlic clove, finely minced

RISO	1½ cups Arborio rice

1. CONDIMENTI: To prepare the artichoke, pull off all the dark green outer leaves until only yellow leaves are exposed. With a knife pare away the remnants of the tough leaves at the base of the artichoke and cut the stem down to the base. Cut 1 to 2 inches off the top of the artichoke to remove any remaining tough or prickly parts. Slice the artichoke lengthwise into halves. With a spoon remove the fuzzy choke. Place each artichoke half, flat side down, on a cutting board. Moving the knife lengthwise across the artichoke, cut each half into thin strips. Squeeze the half-lemon over the sliced artichoke and set aside.

2. BRODO: Bring the broth to a steady simmer in a saucepan on top of the stove.

3. SOFFRITTO: Heat the butter and oil in a heavy 4-quart casserole over moderate heat. Add the onion and garlic and sauté for 1 to 2 minutes, until the onion begins to soften, being careful not to brown it. Add the sliced artichoke and sauté for 2 to 3 minutes longer.

4. RISO: Add the rice to the soffritto; using a wooden spoon, stir for 1 minute, making sure all the grains are well coated. Add the wine and stir until it is completely absorbed. Begin to add the simmering broth, ½ cup at a time, stirring frequently. Wait until each addition is almost completely absorbed before adding the next ½ cup, reserving about ¼ cup to add at the end. Stir frequently to prevent sticking.

5. After approximately 18 minutes, when the rice is tender but still firm, add the reserved broth and the condimenti—the Mascarpone, Parmesan, and parsley—and stir vigorously to combine with the rice. Serve immediately.

Serves 4

VARIATIONS

1. Add ½ cup diced whole-milk mozzarella cheese in place of the Mascarpone cheese.
2. Add 2 tablespoons chopped prosciutto to the soffritto, and substitute an equal amount of red onion for the yellow onion.

Fennel

RISOTTO
AL FINOCCHIO

With its pale green celerylike stalks, fresh fennel's distinctive anise flavor becomes surprisingly subtle when it is cooked. A staple of Italian cooking for centuries, fresh fennel is now widely available in supermarkets throughout the United States, from the late fall until the early spring, where it goes by various names: fennel, the Italian *finocchio,* or, incorrectly, anise, which is a different plant of the same family. Save the fernlike leaves from the fennel stalks for the garnish; they add a dash of bright green color.

BRODO	5 cups Basic Broth (see page 14), approximately
	½ cup dry white wine or broth
SOFFRITTO	2 tablespoons unsalted butter
	1 tablespoon oil
	⅓ cup finely minced onion
	1 celery rib, finely minced
	1 garlic clove, finely minced
RISO	1½ cups Arborio rice
CONDIMENTI	4 ounces, or ½ small bulb, fresh fennel, fernlike tops removed, bulb cut into thin slices, ½-inch long
	1 tablespoon unsalted butter
	⅓ cup grated Parmesan cheese
	1 tablespoon finely minced fennel leaves

1. BRODO: Bring the broth to a steady simmer in a saucepan on top of the stove.

2. SOFFRITTO: Heat the butter and oil in a heavy 4-quart casserole over moderate heat. Add the onion, celery, and garlic, and sauté for 1 to 2 minutes, until the onion begins to soften, being careful not to brown it.

3. RISO: Add the rice to the soffritto; using a wooden spoon, stir for 1 minute, making sure all the grains are well coated. Add the wine and stir until it is completely absorbed.

4. CONDIMENTI: Add the fennel bulb pieces and begin to add the simmering broth, ½ cup at a time, stirring frequently to prevent sticking. Wait until each addition is almost completely absorbed before adding the next ½ cup, reserving about ¼ cup to add at the end. Stir frequently to prevent sticking.

5. After approximately 18 minutes, when the rice is tender but still firm, add the reserved broth. Turn off the heat and add the remaining condimenti—butter and Parmesan—and stir vigorously to combine with the rice. Serve immediately. Garnish with minced fennel leaves.

Serves 4

VARIATION

Add ¾ cup drained plum tomatoes with the fennel in step 4.

Broccoli & Fennel

RISOTTO
CON BROCCOLI E FINOCCHI

The flavor of the broccoli combines with the delicate anise taste of the fennel in surprising harmony. Steamed and puréed, these two green cousins create a creamy combination that makes this an extraordinary risotto.

CONDIMENTI	4 ounces fresh fennel bulbs, fernlike tops removed, cut into 1-inch pieces
	4 ounces broccoli, including peeled stems, leaves, and flowerets, cut into small pieces
	¼ cup light cream
	⅓ cup grated Parmesan cheese
	Salt and freshly ground black pepper
BRODO	5½ cups Basic Broth (see page 14), approximately
SOFFRITTO	2 tablespoons unsalted butter
	1 tablespoon oil
	⅓ cup finely minced onion
	1 garlic clove, finely minced
RISO	1½ cups Arborio rice

1. CONDIMENTI: Add the fennel to a large saucepan of boiling salted water and simmer for 15 minutes. Add the broccoli to the fennel and continue cooking for about 10 minutes longer, until both vegetables are tender. Strain the vegetables. Put the fennel and broccoli, with ¼ cup of the cooking liquid, in a food processor or blender and purée. Add salt and pepper to taste. Set aside.

2. *BRODO:* Bring the broth to a steady simmer in a saucepan on top of the stove.

3. *SOFFRITTO:* Heat the butter and oil in a heavy 4-quart casserole over moderate heat. Add the onion and garlic and sauté for 1 to 2 minutes, until the onion begins to soften, being careful not to brown it.

4. *RISO:* Add the rice to the soffritto; using a wooden spoon, stir for 1 minute, making sure all the grains are well coated. Begin to add the simmering broth, ½ cup at a time, stirring frequently. Wait until each addition is almost completely absorbed before adding the next ½ cup, reserving about ¼ cup to add at the end. Stir frequently to prevent sticking.

5. After approximately 18 minutes, when the rice is tender but still firm, add the reserved broth and the condimenti—fennel and broccoli purée, cream, and Parmesan—and stir vigorously to combine with the rice. Serve immediately.

Serves 4

Lettuce

RISOTTO
CON LA LATTUGA

The sautéed lettuce in this risotto reveals an unexpected depth of flavor that will surprise even the most serious salad eaters. We recommend Boston, Bibb, or Romaine (Roman) lettuce, the varieties most similar to those found in Italy. They lend a particularly fresh taste and bright green color. Iceberg lettuce is not an acceptable substitute in this recipe. Serve before a main course of grilled chicken breasts marinated in olive oil, rosemary, and peperoncino.

CONDIMENTI	1 head of Boston, Bibb, or Romaine lettuce (approximately 3 cups shredded)
	2 tablespoons unsalted butter
	¼ cup light cream
	1 tablespoon chopped fresh parsley
	¼ cup grated Parmesan cheese
BRODO	5 cups Basic Broth (see page 14), approximately
	½ cup dry white wine or broth
SOFFRITTO	2 tablespoons unsalted butter
	1 tablespoon oil
	⅓ cup finely minced onion
	1 garlic clove, finely minced
RISO	1½ cups Arborio rice

1. *CONDIMENTI:* Remove the core and white spine from each leaf of lettuce. Wash and dry the leaves thoroughly, and shred them with a knife. Heat the butter in a small skillet over low heat. Add the lettuce and cook while stirring for about 1 minute, until the leaves are wilted. Turn off the heat and set aside.

2. *BRODO:* Bring the broth to a steady simmer in a saucepan on top of the stove.

3. *SOFFRITTO:* Heat the butter and oil in a heavy 4-quart casserole over moderate heat. Add the onion and garlic and sauté for 1 to 2 minutes, until the onion begins to soften, being careful not to brown it.

4. *RISO:* Add the rice to the soffritto; using a wooden spoon, stir for 1 minute, making sure all the grains are well coated. Add the wine and stir until it is completely absorbed. Begin to add the simmering broth, ½ cup at a time, stirring frequently. Wait until each addition is almost completely absorbed before adding the next ½ cup, reserving about ¼ cup to add at the end. Stir frequently to prevent sticking.

5. After approximately 18 minutes, when the rice is tender but still firm, add the reserved broth and the condimenti—lettuce, cream, parsley, and Parmesan—and stir vigorously to combine with the rice. Serve immediately.

Serves 4

VARIATION

In Lombardy, a lettuce risotto has the addition of peas and asparagus tips. Follow the directions above. In step 1, add ½ cup fresh peas (or defrosted frozen baby peas, not cooked) and the tips from 12 asparagus spears to the sautéed lettuce and continue with the directions.

Leeks

RISOTTO
CON I PORRI

Leek mythology: The Roman Emperor Nero ate leek soup every day to make his voice clear and melodic for delivering long orations.

Leeks and cream make a delicious combination for risotto and will send you singing for seconds. Don't forget to wash the leeks well. Slice them lengthwise into halves and rinse between the layers before cutting. Serve before an entrée of lamb chops in a mustard and caper sauce.

CONDIMENTI	1 tablespoon unsalted butter
	2 or 3 leeks, white part only, cleaned and cut into julienne strips, to make approximately 2 cups
	½ cup light cream
	Salt and freshly ground black pepper
	⅓ cup grated Parmesan cheese
	1 tablespoon chopped fresh parsley
BRODO	5 cups Basic Broth (see page 14), approximately
	½ cup dry white wine or broth
SOFFRITTO	2 tablespoons unsalted butter
	1 tablespoon oil
	⅓ cup finely minced onion
RISO	1½ cups Arborio rice

1. *CONDIMENTI:* Heat the butter in a skillet over moderate heat. When it begins to foam, add the leeks and cook for about 5 minutes, until they are wilted and tender. Add the cream and continue cooking for a few minutes longer, until the cream has thickened. Add salt and pepper to taste. Set aside.

2. *BRODO:* Bring the broth to a steady simmer in a saucepan on top of the stove.

3. *SOFFRITTO:* Heat the butter and oil in a heavy 4-quart casserole over moderate heat. Add the onion and sauté for 1 to 2 minutes, until it begins to soften, being careful not to brown it.

4. *RISO:* Add the rice to the soffritto; using a wooden spoon, stir for 1 minute, making sure all the grains are well coated. Add the wine and stir until it is completely absorbed. Begin to add the simmering broth, ½ cup at a time, stirring frequently. Wait until each addition is almost completely absorbed before adding the next ½ cup. Stir frequently to prevent sticking.

5. After approximately 18 minutes, when the rice is tender but still firm, add the condimenti—leeks and cream, Parmesan, and parsley—and stir vigorously to combine with the rice. Serve immediately.

Serves 4

VARIATION

Add 2 tablespoons chopped pancetta and ¼ cup tomato, peeled, seeded, and diced, to the leeks. Omit the parsley.

Peas

RISOTTO
CON PISELLI

One of the most celebrated Venetian specialties, Risi e Bisi (Venetian dialect for "rice and peas") was the traditional dish served to the Doges on the day of St. Mark, the patron saint of Venice. Risi e Bisi, a *minestra* or thick soup, is the inspiration for this risotto of elegant simplicity: a basic risotto brimming with tender sweet young peas. We like to sauté the peas gently in a bit of butter and add them in at the very end. This ensures that they keep their bright green color and firm texture.

CONDIMENTI	1 tablespoon unsalted butter
	1 cup shelled fresh peas or defrosted frozen peas, not cooked
	¼ cup light cream
	⅓ cup grated Parmesan cheese
BRODO	5 cups Basic Broth (see page 14), approximately
	½ cup dry white wine or broth
SOFFRITTO	2 tablespoons unsalted butter
	1 tablespoon oil
	⅓ cup finely minced onion
	1 celery rib, finely minced
RISO	1½ cups Arborio rice

1. *CONDIMENTI:* Heat the butter in a small skillet over moderate heat. When it begins to foam, add the peas and cook for 3 to 5 minutes, stirring occasionally. Turn off heat and set aside.

2. *BRODO:* Bring the broth to a steady simmer in a saucepan on top of the stove.

3. *SOFFRITTO:* Heat the butter and oil in a heavy 4-quart casserole over moderate heat. Add the onion and celery and sauté for 1 to 2 minutes, until the onion begins to soften, being careful not to brown it.

4. *RISO:* Add the rice to the soffritto; using a wooden spoon, stir for 1 minute, making sure all the grains are well coated. Add the wine and stir until it is completely absorbed. Begin to add the simmering broth, ½ cup at a time, stirring frequently. Wait until each addition is almost completely absorbed before adding the next ½ cup, reserving about ¼ cup to add at the end. Stir frequently to prevent sticking.

5. After approximately 18 minutes, when the rice is tender but still firm, add the reserved broth and the condimenti—peas, cream, and Parmesan—and stir vigorously to combine with the rice. Serve immediately.

Serves 4

VARIATIONS

1. Add 1 tablespoon diced prosciutto to the soffritto.

2. To intensify the pea flavor, cook the peas in the broth while you are preparing the risotto, for 10 to 15 minutes. Strain the peas, purée them in a food processor or blender, and add them to the risotto in step 5.

Zucchini

RISOTTO
CON ZUCCHINE ALLA VENETA

The Veneto, the region that stretches from Venice on the Adriatic to the mountainous villages of the Swiss Alps, has a culinary tradition as diverse as its terrain, yet it is well known for its simplicity: for using basic ingredients in uncomplicated preparations. Zucchini sautéed with garlic and oil couldn't be simpler, and when it is added to risotto, it couldn't be more delicious.

CONDIMENTI	2 medium-size zucchini, about 1 pound
	1 tablespoon oil
	1 large or 2 small garlic cloves, finely minced
	1 tablespoon chopped fresh parsley
	⅓ cup grated Parmesan cheese
BRODO	5 cups Basic Broth (see page 14), approximately
	½ cup dry white wine or broth
SOFFRITTO	3 tablespoons oil
	⅓ cup finely minced onion
RISO	1½ cups Arborio rice

1. CONDIMENTI: Wash the zucchini, remove the stems, and coarsely grate or cut into small julienne strips. Heat the oil in a skillet over moderate heat, add the garlic and zucchini, and cook for 5 minutes, or until zucchini are tender. Turn off the heat and set aside.

2. *BRODO:* Bring the broth to a steady simmer in a saucepan on top of the stove.

3. *SOFFRITTO:* Heat the oil in a heavy 4-quart casserole over moderate heat. Add the onion and sauté for 1 to 2 minutes, until it begins to soften, being careful not to brown it.

4. *RISO:* Add the rice to the soffritto; using a wooden spoon, stir for 1 minute, making sure all the grains are well coated. Add the wine and stir until it is completely absorbed. Begin to add the simmering broth, ½ cup at a time, stirring frequently. Wait until each addition is almost completely absorbed before adding the next ½ cup, reserving about ¼ cup to add at the end. Stir frequently to prevent sticking. Add the zucchini after the rice has been cooking for 10 minutes.

5. After approximately 18 minutes, when the rice is tender but still firm, add the reserved broth. Turn off the heat and add the remaining condimenti—parsley and Parmesan—and stir vigorously to combine with the rice. Serve immediately.

Serves 4

VARIATION

Add 2 tablespoons chopped pancetta to the soffritto.

Zucchini & Mozzarella Cheese

RISOTTO
CON ZUCCHINE E MOZZARELLA

This risotto is one of our favorite late summer dishes when zucchini season comes around. Serve this risotto as a second course after an antipasto of thin-sliced prosciutto and fresh figs or melon, and with a fruity red wine like Valpolicella.

CONDIMENTI	1 tablespoon unsalted butter
	1 medium-size zucchini, washed, cut lengthwise into halves, and sliced into half-rounds
	3 ounces mozzarella cheese, cut into cubes
	¼ cup light cream
	1 tablespoon chopped fresh parsley
	¼ cup grated Parmesan cheese
BRODO	5 cups Basic Broth (see page 14), approximately
	½ cup dry white wine or broth
SOFFRITTO	2 tablespoons unsalted butter
	1 tablespoon oil
	⅓ cup finely minced onion
	1 garlic clove, finely minced
RISO	1½ cups Arborio rice

1. CONDIMENTI: Heat the butter in a small skillet over moderate heat. When it begins to foam, add the sliced zucchini. Cook, stirring frequently, until zucchini becomes tender, in 5 to 7 minutes. Turn off the heat and set aside.

2. BRODO: Bring the broth to a steady simmer in a saucepan on top of the stove.

3. SOFFRITTO: Heat the butter and oil in a heavy 4-quart casserole over moderate heat. Add the onion and garlic and sauté for 1 to 2 minutes, until the onion begins to soften, being careful not to brown it.

4. RISO: Add the rice to the soffritto; using a wooden spoon, stir for 1 minute, making sure all the grains are well coated. Add the wine and stir until it is completely absorbed. Begin to add the simmering broth, ½ cup at a time, stirring frequently. Wait until each addition is almost completely absorbed before adding the next ½ cup, reserving about ¼ cup to add at the end. Stir frequently to prevent sticking.

5. After approximately 18 minutes, when the rice is tender but still firm, add the reserved broth and the condimenti—zucchini, mozzarella, cream, parsley, and Parmesan—and stir vigorously to combine with the rice. Serve immediately.

Serves 4

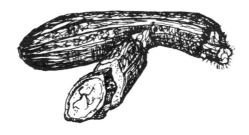

VARIATION

Add chopped fresh basil in place of the parsley in step 5.

Parsley

RISOTTO
AL PREZZEMOLO

Parsley departs from its traditional role as a garnish to take center stage in this risotto. We like to use fresh flat-leaf (Italian) parsley; it has a zestier flavor than its curly counterpart. This is a great palate opener for almost any main course to follow. Try it before a stew of fresh fish, seafood, and tomatoes.

BRODO	5 cups Basic Broth (see page 14), approximately
	½ cup dry white wine or broth
SOFFRITTO	2 tablespoons unsalted butter
	1 tablespoon oil
	⅓ cup finely minced onion
RISO	1½ cups Arborio rice
CONDIMENTI	1 bunch of parsley, washed, thickest stems removed, chopped to make ¾ to 1 cup (see Index for Parsley)
	1 tablespoon unsalted butter
	¼ cup grated Parmesan cheese

1. BRODO: Bring the broth to a steady simmer in a saucepan on top of the stove.
2. SOFFRITTO: Heat the butter and oil in a heavy 4-quart casse-

role over moderate heat. Add the onion and sauté for 1 to 2 minutes, until it begins to soften, being careful not to brown it.

3. *RISO:* Add the rice to the soffritto; using a wooden spoon, stir for 1 minute, making sure all the grains are well coated. Add the wine and stir until it is completely absorbed. Begin to add the simmering broth, ½ cup at a time, stirring frequently. Wait until each addition is almost completely absorbed before adding the next ½ cup, reserving about ¼ cup to add at the end. Stir frequently to prevent sticking.

4. *CONDIMENTI:* After approximately 18 minutes, when the rice is tender but still firm, add the reserved broth and the parsley. Turn off the heat and add the remaining condimenti—butter and Parmesan—and stir vigorously to combine with the rice. Serve immediately.

Serves 4

VARIATION

Add ¼ cup Mascarpone cheese in place of the butter in the condimenti.

Fresh Herbs

RISOTTO
ALLE ERBE

In this risotto you can create the blend of herbs that suits your own taste. We like a combination of equal parts basil and parsley with just a hint of rosemary, or equal parts basil, marjoram, and oregano. Using all rosemary is classically done in Italy. The key to success is the freshness of the herbs. Dried substitutes do not lend the right flavor. This risotto is so versatile that it can precede almost any entrée. Serve it before a dinner of cold poached fish and grilled zucchini.

BRODO	5 cups Basic Broth (see page 14), approximately
	½ cup dry white wine or broth
SOFFRITTO	2 tablespoons unsalted butter
	1 tablespoon oil
	⅓ cup finely minced onion
	2 tablespoons finely minced celery
RISO	1½ cups Arborio rice
CONDIMENTI	1 cup finely chopped fresh herbs, such as basil, parsley, rosemary, oregano, marjoram, and thyme
	1 tablespoon unsalted butter
	⅓ cup grated Parmesan cheese

1. BRODO: Bring the broth to a steady simmer in a saucepan on top of the stove.

2. SOFFRITTO: Heat the butter and oil in a heavy 4-quart casserole over moderate heat. Add the onion and celery and sauté for 1 to 2 minutes, until the onion begins to soften, being careful not to brown it.

3. RISO: Add the rice to the soffritto; using a wooden spoon, stir for 1 minute, making sure all the grains are well coated. Add the wine and stir until it is completely absorbed. Begin to add the simmering broth, ½ cup at a time, stirring frequently. Wait until each addition is almost completely absorbed before adding the next ½ cup, reserving about ¼ cup to add at the end. Stir frequently to prevent sticking.

4. CONDIMENTI: After approximately 18 minutes, when the rice is tender but still firm, add the reserved broth and the herb mixture. Turn off the heat and add the remaining condimenti—butter and Parmesan—and stir vigorously to combine with the rice. Serve immediately.

Serves 4

Pesto

RISOTTO AL PESTO

Pesto, a fresh basil and pine nut sauce, has become almost synonymous with Italian cooking in recent years. Happily, we found that pesto does as much for risotto as it does for pasta.

BRODO	5½ cups Basic Broth (see page 14), approximately
SOFFRITTO	2 tablespoons unsalted butter
	1 tablespoon oil
	⅓ cup finely minced onion
RISO	1½ cups Arborio rice
CONDIMENTI	½ cup prepared Pesto (recipe follows)
	1 tablespoon unsalted butter
	4 tablespoons pine nuts, for garnish

1. BRODO: Bring the broth to a steady simmer in a saucepan on top of the stove.

2. SOFFRITTO: Heat the butter and oil in a heavy 4-quart casserole over moderate heat. Add the onion and sauté for 1 to 2 minutes, until it begins to soften, being careful not to brown it.

3. RISO: Add the rice to the soffritto; using a wooden spoon, stir for 1 minute, making sure all the grains are well coated. Begin to add the simmering broth, ½ cup at a time, stirring frequently. Wait until each addition is almost completely absorbed before adding the next ½ cup, reserving about ¼ cup to add at the end. Stir frequently to prevent sticking.

4. CONDIMENTI: After approximately 18 minutes, when the rice is tender but still firm, add the reserved broth and the condimenti—the prepared Pesto. Turn off the heat and add the butter, and stir vigorously to combine with the rice. Garnish each serving with pine nuts. Serve immediately.

Serves 4

Pesto

1 cup loosely packed fresh basil leaves, washed

1 garlic clove, peeled

1 tablespoon pine nuts (if not available, use walnuts)

¼ cup olive oil

¼ teaspoon salt

⅓ cup grated Parmesan cheese

2 tablespoons grated Pecorino Romano cheese

1. Combine basil, garlic, pine nuts, oil, and salt in the bowl of a food processor or a blender. Process until smooth.

2. Stir in the Parmesan and Romano cheeses, and add to risotto in step 4.

Makes about ½ cup

1. Spinach pesto can also be used, for a milder flavor. Substitute an equal amount of spinach for the basil in the pesto recipe.

2. If using store-bought pesto, make sure it's of high quality. Depending on the brand, you may want to add some Parmesan or Pecorino to the risotto in step 4.

Watercress & Taleggio Cheese

RISOTTO
AL CRESCIONE E TALEGGIO

In this risotto, the crisp, peppery flavor of the watercress is complemented by the mellow taste of the Taleggio. We omit the customary last ¼ cup of broth at the end of cooking because the fresh watercress and Taleggio produce enough extra liquid to give this dish a perfect creamy consistency.

BRODO	5½ cups Basic Broth (see page 14), approximately
SOFFRITTO	2 tablespoons unsalted butter
	1 tablespoon oil
	⅓ cup finely minced onion
RISO	1½ cups Arborio rice

CONDIMENTI	1 bunch of watercress, washed, thickest stems removed, chopped
	4 ounces Taleggio cheese, rind removed, cut into pieces
	1 tablespoon unsalted butter
	¼ cup grated Parmesan cheese

1. BRODO: Bring the broth to a steady simmer in a saucepan on top of the stove.

2. SOFFRITTO: Heat the butter and oil in a heavy 4-quart casserole over moderate heat. Add the onion and sauté for 1 to 2 minutes, until it begins to soften, being careful not to brown it.

3. RISO: Add the rice to the soffritto; using a wooden spoon, stir for 1 minute, making sure all the grains are well coated. Begin to add the simmering broth, ½ cup at a time, stirring frequently. Wait until each addition is almost completely absorbed before adding the next ½ cup until all the broth has been added. Stir frequently to prevent sticking.

4. CONDIMENTI: Add the watercress after the rice has been cooking for 10 minutes and continue to add the broth, ½ cup at a time.

5. After approximately 18 minutes, when the rice is tender but still firm, turn off the heat and add the remaining condimenti—Taleggio, butter, and Parmesan—and stir vigorously to combine with the rice. Serve immediately.

Serves 4

VARIATION

If you cannot find Taleggio cheese in your store, substitute Italian Fontina or mozzarella.

Colorful Risotti

Tomatoes

RISOTTO CON I POMODORI

Southern Italian cooking wouldn't exist without tomatoes, but in Northern Italy tomatoes are mostly used sparingly for a touch of added flavor and color. In this risotto we use only fresh, ripe, small, preferably plum, tomatoes. They add a light, delicate tomato taste. For a stronger tomato flavor you can use well-drained canned tomatoes. We like to add some fresh basil, but when it is not available, we use dried basil or fresh parsley.

CONDIMENTI   3 plum tomatoes, peeled, seeded, and chopped, or ¾ cup canned Italian tomatoes, well drained and chopped

2 tablespoons unsalted butter

Salt and freshly ground black pepper

⅓ cup grated Parmesan cheese

1 tablespoon minced fresh basil

BRODO	5 cups Basic Broth (see page 14), approximately
	½ cup dry white wine or broth

SOFFRITTO	2 tablespoons unsalted butter
	1 tablespoon oil
	⅓ cup finely minced onion

RISO	1½ cups Arborio rice

1. CONDIMENTI: To prepare the fresh tomatoes, drop them into boiling salted water (the salt helps to retain the red color) for 30 seconds, then immediately run them under cold water. With a knife peel the skins off and scrape out the seeds with a spoon, or squeeze the tomatoes to remove the cores. Coarsely chop the tomatoes. Heat the butter in a skillet over moderate heat and add the tomatoes. Cook for 2 to 3 minutes, until the tomatoes become tender and turn a red-orange color. Add salt and pepper to taste. Turn off the heat and set aside.

2. BRODO: Bring the broth to a steady simmer in a saucepan on top of the stove.

3. SOFFRITTO: Heat the butter and oil in a heavy 4-quart casserole over moderate heat. Add the onion and sauté for 1 to 2 minutes, until it begins to soften, being careful not to brown it.

4. RISO: Add the rice to the soffritto; using a wooden spoon, stir for 1 minute, making sure all the grains are well coated. Add the wine and stir until it is completely absorbed. Begin to add the simmering broth, ½ cup at a time, stirring frequently. Wait until each addition is almost completely absorbed before adding the next ½ cup, reserving about ¼ cup to add at the end. Stir frequently to prevent sticking.

5. After approximately 18 minutes, when the rice is tender but still firm, add the reserved broth and the tomatoes. Turn off the heat and immediately add the remaining condimenti—Parmesan and basil—and stir vigorously to combine with the rice. Serve immediately.

Serves 4

VARIATION

Add a pinch of saffron to the rice when you begin to add the broth. It will lend an intense orange hue to the risotto.

Tomato and Mozzarella

RISOTTO
ALLA CAPRESE

This risotto captures the flavors of the classic combination of tomatoes and mozzarella. The mozzarella with the richest flavor is the kind you buy freshly made, but commercially packaged whole-milk mozzarella will work just as well in this recipe. Fresh tomatoes are always our first choice, but when they're not available, canned plum tomatoes will yield fine results. Serve before a loin of pork roasted with fresh herbs and garlic.

BRODO   5 cups Basic Broth (see page 14), approximately

½ cup dry white wine or broth

SOFFRITTO	2 tablespoons unsalted butter
	1 tablespoon oil
	⅓ cup finely minced onion
	2 plum tomatoes, peeled, seeded, and chopped, or ½ cup canned Italian tomatoes, well drained and chopped
RISO	1½ cups Arborio rice
CONDIMENTI	4 ounces mozzarella cheese, cut into small pieces
	1 tablespoon unsalted butter
	1 tablespoon chopped fresh oregano, or ½ teaspoon dried
	¼ cup grated Parmesan cheese
	Salt and freshly ground black pepper

1. BRODO: Bring the broth to a steady simmer in a saucepan on top of the stove.

2. SOFFRITTO: Heat the butter and oil in a heavy 4-quart casserole over moderate heat. Add the onion and tomatoes and sauté for 1 to 2 minutes, until the onion begins to soften, being careful not to brown it.

3. RISO: Add the rice to the soffritto; using a wooden spoon, stir for 1 minute, making sure all the grains are well coated. Add the wine and stir until it is completely absorbed. Begin to add the simmering broth, ½ cup at a time, stirring frequently. Wait until each addition is almost completely absorbed before adding the next ½ cup, reserving about ¼ cup to add at the end. Stir frequently to prevent sticking.

4. CONDIMENTI: After approximately 18 minutes, when the rice is tender but still firm, add the reserved broth. Turn off the heat and immediately add the condimenti—mozzarella, butter, oregano, and Parmesan—and stir vigorously until the cheeses are melted and combined with the rice. Add salt and pepper to taste. Serve immediately.

Serves 4

Tomato Concentrate

RISOTTO ROSSO

The small quantity of tomato paste in this risotto adds just a hint of flavor but a lot of red color. Risotto Rosso is usually served as one part of a Risotti Tricolori (three colors), together with a green risotto, either spinach or parsley, and a white risotto , such as Risotto al Parmigiano (see page 53). You can use any brand of tomato paste with fine results. Imported Italian tomato paste is conveniently available in a tube so you can squeeze out just the right amount. We like to add some chopped fresh parsley to this risotto and serve it as an accompaniment to an entrée of lamb or chicken.

BRODO	5 cups Basic Broth (see page 14), approximately
	1 bay leaf
	½ cup dry white wine or broth
SOFFRITTO	2 tablespoons unsalted butter
	1 tablespoon oil
	⅓ cup finely minced onion
RISO	1½ cups Arborio rice
CONDIMENTI	2 tablespoons tomato paste
	1 tablespoon unsalted butter
	2 tablespoons chopped fresh parsley (optional)
	⅓ cup grated Parmesan cheese

1. BRODO: Bring the broth to a steady simmer in a saucepan on top of the stove.

2. SOFFRITTO: Heat the butter and oil in a heavy 4-quart casserole over moderate heat. Add the onion and sauté for 1 to 2 minutes, until it begins to soften, being careful not to brown it.

3. RISO: Add the rice to the soffritto; using a wooden spoon, stir

for 1 minute, making sure all the grains are well coated. Add the wine and stir until it is completely absorbed. Begin to add the simmering broth, ½ cup at a time, stirring frequently. Wait until each addition is almost completely absorbed before adding the next ½ cup, reserving about ¼ cup to add at the end. Stir frequently to prevent sticking.

4. CONDIMENTI: After approximately 18 minutes, when the rice is tender but still firm, add the reserved broth. Turn off the heat and add the condimenti—tomato paste, butter, parsley, and Parmesan—and stir vigorously to combine with the rice. Serve immediately.

Serves 4

VARIATION

Add 2 tablespoons chopped prosciutto to the soffritto and ¼ teaspoon powdered saffron to the rice in step 3.

Sun-Dried Tomatoes & Fontina

RISOTTO
CON POMODORI SECCHI E FONTINA

The combination of the concentrated flavor of the sun-dried tomatoes with their oil in addition to tomato paste gives this risotto the most intense tomato taste. This is a perfect luncheon main course. Serve it with cold steamed leeks, lightly doused with a dressing of lemon juice, extra-virgin olive oil, salt, and freshly ground black pepper.

BRODO	5 cups Basic Broth (see page 14), approximately
	½ cup dry white wine or broth
SOFFRITTO	2 tablespoons unsalted butter
	1 tablespoon oil from sun-dried tomatoes (see page 45)
	⅓ cup finely minced onion
RISO	1½ cups Arborio rice
CONDIMENTI	⅓ cup coarsely chopped sun-dried tomatoes packed in oil (see page 45)
	1 tablespoon tomato paste
	4 ounces Fontina cheese, rind removed, cut into small pieces
	1 tablespoon chopped fresh parsley
	2 tablespoons grated Parmesan cheese

1. BRODO: Bring the broth to a steady simmer in a saucepan on top of the stove.

2. SOFFRITTO: Heat the butter and oil in a heavy 4-quart casserole over moderate heat. Add the onion and sauté for 1 to 2 minutes, until it begins to soften, being careful not to brown it.

3. RISO: Add the rice to the soffritto; using a wooden spoon, stir for 1 minute, making sure all the grains are well coated. Add the wine and stir until it is completely absorbed. Begin to add the simmering broth, ½ cup at a time, stirring frequently. Wait until each addition is almost completely absorbed before adding the next ½ cup, reserving about ¼ cup to add at the end. Stir frequently to prevent sticking.

4. CONDIMENTI: Add the sun-dried tomatoes and tomato paste after the rice has been cooking for 10 minutes. Continue to add the broth, ½ cup at a time, stirring frequently.

5. After approximately 18 minutes, when the rice is tender but still firm, add the reserved broth and remaining condimenti—Fontina, parsley, and Parmesan—and stir vigorously until the cheeses are melted and combined with the rice. Serve immediately.

Serves 4

Peppers & Tomatoes

RISOTTO
ALLA CREOLA

Creole-style cooking is not generally associated with Italian cuisine, so we were surprised to discover this risotto. The Italians base this dish, not on our Louisiana Creole-style cooking, but on French Caribbean island fare. Add a pinch of dried hot pepper to give this colorful dish even more pizazz. Serve as a main course with a salad of watercress and endive.

CONDIMENTI 1 tablespoon unsalted butter

3 small tomatoes, preferably Italian plum tomatoes, peeled, seeded, and chopped, or ¾ cup canned Italian plum tomatoes, well drained and chopped

½ green bell pepper, cut into julienne strips

½ red bell pepper, cut into julienne strips

Salt and freshly ground black pepper

1 tablespoon chopped fresh parsley

⅓ cup grated Parmesan cheese

BRODO	5 cups Basic Broth (see page 14), approximately
	½ teaspoon powdered saffron
	½ cup dry white wine

SOFFRITTO	2 tablespoons unsalted butter
	1 tablespoon oil
	⅓ cup finely minced onion
	1 garlic clove, finely minced

RISO	1½ cups Arborio rice

1. CONDIMENTI: Heat the butter in a small skillet over moderate heat. When it begins to foam, add the tomatoes and peppers and cook for about 5 minutes, until the tomatoes lose their red color and the peppers become tender. Add salt and pepper to taste. Turn off heat and set aside.

2. BRODO: Bring the broth combined with the saffron to a steady simmer in a saucepan on top of the stove.

3. SOFFRITTO: Heat the butter and oil in a heavy 4-quart casserole over moderate heat. Add the onion and garlic and sauté for 1 to 2 minutes, until the onion begins to soften, being careful not to brown it.

4. RISO: Add the rice to the soffritto; using a wooden spoon, stir for 1 minute, making sure all the grains are well coated. Add the wine and stir until it is completely absorbed. Begin to add the simmering broth, ½ cup at a time, stirring frequently. Wait until each addition is almost completely absorbed before adding the next ½ cup, reserving about ¼ cup to add at the end. Stir frequently to prevent sticking.

5. After approximately 18 minutes, when the rice is tender but still firm, add the reserved broth. Turn off the heat and immediately add the condimenti—tomatoes and peppers, parsley, and Parmesan—and stir vigorously to combine with the rice. Serve immediately.

Serves 4

Green, Red, & Yellow Peppers

RISOTTO
AI PEPERONI TRICOLORI

The confetti of diced peppers makes this a festive as well as flavorful risotto. Feel free to alter the amount of each type of pepper to your liking. For a delicious vegetarian dinner we like to serve this risotto before eggplant prepared *alla milanese,* sliced, dipped into egg and bread crumbs, and fried in hot oil.

CONDIMENTI	2 tablespoons unsalted butter
	1 cup diced sweet bell peppers (¾ cup each of green, red, and yellow pepper), seeds and stems removed (see Note)
	Salt and freshly ground black pepper
	⅓ cup grated Parmesan cheese
	1 tablespoon chopped fresh parsley
BRODO	5 cups Basic Broth (see page 14), approximately
	½ cup dry white wine or broth
SOFFRITTO	2 tablespoons unsalted butter
	1 tablespoon oil
	⅓ cup finely minced onion
	1 garlic clove, finely minced
RISO	1½ cups Arborio rice

1. CONDIMENTI: Heat the butter in a small skillet over moderate heat. When it begins to foam, add the diced peppers and gently sauté, stirring frequently, for about 5 minutes. Do not brown. Add salt and pepper to taste. Set aside.

2. BRODO: Bring the broth to a steady simmer in a saucepan on top of the stove.

3. SOFFRITTO: Heat the butter and oil in a heavy 4-quart casserole over moderate heat. Add the onion and garlic and sauté for 1 to 2 minutes, until the onion begins to soften, being careful not to brown it.

4. RISO: Add the rice to the soffritto; using a wooden spoon, stir for 1 minute, making sure all the grains are well coated. Add the wine and stir until it is almost completely absorbed. Begin to add the simmering broth, ½ cup at a time, stirring frequently. Wait until each addition is almost completely absorbed before adding the next ½ cup, reserving about ¼ cup to add at the end. Stir frequently to prevent sticking.

5. After approximately 18 minutes, when the rice is tender but still firm, add the reserved broth. Turn off the heat and immediately add the condimenti—peppers, Parmesan, and parsley—and stir vigorously to combine with the rice. Serve immediately.

Serves 4

NOTE: The freshest peppers are always firm and glossy. Avoid any that are wrinkled or bruised.

VARIATION

For a more intense sweet pepper taste, roast the peppers over the stove flame or under the oven broiler, turning frequently, until they are completely blackened. Run them under cold water to remove the charred skin. Cut into halves to remove the core and seeds, dice, and add to the risotto in step 5 with the condimenti and 1 tablespoon unsalted butter.

Zucchini & Tomatoes

RISOTTO
CON ZUCCHINE E POMODORI

Here's a savory solution for your garden-fresh summer zucchini and to-matoes. This risotto makes a satisfying luncheon or light supper entrée. Serve it with some crusty bread and a salad of crisp cold greens.

CONDIMENTI	1 medium-size zucchini
	1 tablespoon unsalted butter
	2 small tomatoes, peeled, seeded, and chopped, or ½ cup canned Italian toma-toes, well drained and chopped
	2 ounces Fontina cheese, cut into small pieces
	1 tablespoon chopped fresh parsley
	¼ cup grated Parmesan cheese
BRODO	5 cups Basic Broth (see page 14), approxi-mately
	½ cup dry white wine or broth
SOFFRITTO	2 tablespoons unsalted butter
	1 tablespoon oil
	⅓ cup finely minced onion
	1 tablespoon finely chopped prosciutto (op-tional)
RISO	1½ cups Arborio rice

1. CONDIMENTI: Wash the zucchini, trim the stem, and dice. Heat the butter in a skillet over moderate heat. Add the zucchini and tomatoes and gently sauté until the zucchini is tender, about 5 minutes. Turn off heat and set aside.

2. BRODO: Bring the broth to a steady simmer in a saucepan on top of the stove.

3. SOFFRITTO: Heat the butter and oil in a heavy 4-quart casserole over moderate heat. Add the onion and prosciutto and sauté for 1 to 2 minutes, until the onion begins to soften, being careful not to brown it.

4. RISO: Add the rice to the soffritto; using a wooden spoon, stir for 1 minute, making sure all the grains are well coated. Add the wine and stir until it is completely absorbed. Begin to add the simmering broth, ½ cup at a time, stirring frequently. Wait until each addition is almost completely absorbed before adding the next ½ cup, reserving about ¼ cup to add at the end. Stir frequently to prevent sticking.

5. After approximately 18 minutes, when the rice is tender but still firm, add the reserved broth and the condimenti—the zucchini and tomato mixture, Fontina, parsley, and Parmesan—and stir vigorously until the cheeses are melted and combined with the rice. Serve immediately.

Serves 4

VARIATION

Mozzarella cheese can be substituted for the Fontina.

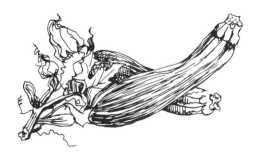

Zucchini Blossoms

RISOTTO
AI FIORE DI ZUCCA

The bright yellow blossoms that grow at the tips of zucchini, with their mild, fresh flavor and soft, leafy texture, are a common ingredient in risotti. This risotto with squash blossoms, which can be served with a garnish of fresh white truffle, is our version of one we sampled at the Milanese restaurant Da Aimo e Nadia. We follow their instructions to leave the blossoms whole and add them to the risotto a few at a time as the rice cooks. Squash blossoms are a familiar sight in Italian markets, but unfortunately they are practically unknown commercially in the United States. For this risotto, you'll have to find a home-grown source for your zucchini blossoms. We can assure you it's well worth the search.

BRODO	5½ cups Basic Broth (see page 14), approximately
	½ cup dry white wine
SOFFRITTO	2 tablespoons unsalted butter
	1 tablespoon oil
	3 tablespoons finely minced onion
	2 tablespoons chopped fresh parsley
RISO	1½ cups Arborio rice
CONDIMENTI	10 to 20 squash blossoms, washed, stems and pistils removed (reserve 2 blossoms, coarsely chopped, for garnish)

1 tablespoon unsalted butter

¼ cup grated Parmesan cheese

1 fresh white truffle, grated, for garnish (see
  Index for White Truffle Risotto, optional)

1. BRODO: Bring the broth to a steady simmer in a saucepan on top of the stove.

2. SOFFRITTO: Heat the butter and oil in a heavy 4-quart casserole over moderate heat. Add the onion and parsley and saute for 1 to 2 minutes, until the onion begins to soften, being careful not to brown it.

3. RISO: Add the rice to the soffritto; using a wooden spoon, stir for 1 minute, making sure all the grains are well coated. Add the wine and stir until it is completely absorbed. Begin to add the simmering broth, ½ cup at a time, stirring frequently. Wait until each addition is almost completely absorbed before adding the next ½ cup, reserving about ¼ cup to add at the end. Stir frequently to prevent sticking.

4. CONDIMENTI: Add 6 squash blossoms after the rice has been cooking for 5 minutes. Add 6 more blossoms after the rice has been cooking for 10 minutes.

5. After approximately 18 minutes, when the rice is tender but still firm, add the reserved broth and remaining 6 squash blossoms. Turn off the heat and immediately add the remaining condimenti—butter and Parmesan—and stir vigorously to combine with the rice. Serve immediately. Garnish each serving with grated truffle (if available) and chopped squash blossoms.

Serves 4

VARIATION

Add 2 tablespoons chopped prosciutto to the soffritto.

Eggplant

RISSOTO
ALLE MELANZANE

This is our adaptation of a favorite pasta dish that calls for eggplant, tomatoes, and penne baked together with mozzarella. The same combination of flavors is also great in risotto; here the rice, not the pasta, creates a natural background for the other ingredients. The eggplant picks up the taste of the tomatoes, and the mozzarella makes the final result rich and creamy.

CONDIMENTI

2 cups eggplant, peeled and cubed

1 tablespoon salt

1 tablespoon olive oil

1 tablespoon unsalted butter

2 small tomatoes, peeled, seeded, and chopped, or ½ cup canned Italian plum tomatoes, well drained and coarsely chopped

½ cup diced mozzarella cheese

¼ cup grated Parmesan cheese

1 tablespoon chopped fresh parsley

BRODO	5 cups Basic Broth (see page 14), approximately
	½ cup dry white wine or broth

SOFFRITTO	2 tablespoons unsalted butter
	1 tablespoon oil
	⅓ cup finely minced onion

RISO	1½ cups Arborio rice

1. CONDIMENTI: Put the eggplant cubes in a colander. Sprinkle with 1 tablespoon salt and allow to stand for 30 minutes. Pat dry with paper towel. Heat the olive oil and butter in a skillet over moderate heat; when the butter begins to foam, add the eggplant and tomatoes and cook for 5 to 10 minutes, until the eggplant is tender. Turn off heat and set aside.

2. BRODO: Bring the broth to a steady simmer in a saucepan on top of the stove.

3. SOFFRITTO: Heat the butter and oil in a heavy 4-quart casserole over moderate heat. Add the onion and sauté for 1 to 2 minutes, until it begins to soften, being careful not to brown it.

4. RISO: Add the rice to the soffritto; using a wooden spoon, stir for 1 minute, making sure all the grains are well coated. Add the wine and stir until it is completely absorbed. Begin to add the simmering broth, ½ cup at a time, stirring frequently. Wait until each addition is almost completely absorbed before adding the next ½ cup, reserving about ¼ cup to add at the end. Stir frequently to prevent sticking.

5. After approximately 18 minutes, when the rice is tender but still firm, add the reserved broth and the condimenti—eggplant and tomatoes, mozzarella, Parmesan, and parsley—and stir vigorously until the cheeses are melted and combined with the rice. Serve immediately.

Serves 4

Carrots & Cream

RISOTTO
CON CAROTE E PANNA

Carrots and cream make a great combination that is colorful and rich with just a hint of sweetness; the bright orange of the carrots is highlighted by the flourish of green parsley. Serve this risotto before an entrée of highly seasoned roast chicken with a mustard, garlic, and ginger coating.

BRODO	5 cups Basic Broth (see page 14), approximately
	½ cup dry white wine or broth
SOFFRITTO	2 tablespoons unsalted butter
	1 tablespoon oil
	⅓ cup finely minced onion
CONDIMENTI	1 cup coarsely grated peeled carrot or cut into thin julienne strips
	½ cup light cream
	⅓ cup grated Parmesan cheese
	1 tablespoon chopped fresh parsley
RISO	1½ cups Arborio rice

1. BRODO: Bring the broth to a steady simmer in a saucepan on top of the stove.

2. SOFFRITTO: Heat the butter and oil in a heavy 4-quart casse-

role over moderate heat. Add the onion and sauté for 1 to 2 minutes, until it begins to soften, being careful not to brown it.

3. _CONDIMENTI:_ Add the carrots to the soffritto and cook for 2 to 3 minutes.

4. _RISO:_ Add the rice to soffritto and carrots; using a wooden spoon, stir for 1 minute, making sure all the grains are well coated. Add the wine and stir until it is completely absorbed. Begin to add the simmering broth, ½ cup at a time, stirring frequently. Wait until each addition is almost completely absorbed before adding the next ½ cup, reserving about ¼ cup to add at the end. Stir frequently to prevent sticking.

5. After approximately 18 minutes, when the rice is tender but still firm, add the reserved broth and remaining condimenti—cream, Parmesan, and parsley—and stir vigorously to combine with the rice. Serve immediately.

Serves 4

Beets

RISOTTO
ROSA

The intense pink *(rosa)* from the beets and the bright green of the parsley create a striking risotto. Serve before an entrée of cornish game hens roasted with sage and olives.

BRODO	5 cups Basic Broth (see page 14), approximately
	½ cup dry white wine or broth
SOFFRITTO	2 tablespoons unsalted butter
	1 tablespoon oil
	⅓ cup finely minced onion
RISO	1½ cups Arborio rice
CONDIMENTI	2 whole fresh beets, green tops removed, washed, peeled, and diced (about 1 cup)
	¼ cup light cream
	⅓ cup grated Parmesan cheese
	1 tablespoon chopped fresh parsley

1. BRODO: Bring the broth to a steady simmer in a saucepan on top of the stove.

2. SOFFRITTO: Heat the butter and oil in a heavy 4-quart casserole over moderate heat. Add the onion and sauté for 1 to 2 minutes,

until it begins to soften, being careful not to brown it.

3. *RISO:* Add the rice to the soffritto; using a wooden spoon, stir for 1 minute, making sure all the grains are well coated. Add the wine and stir until it is completely absorbed.

4. *CONDIMENTI:* Add the diced beets. Begin to add the simmering broth, ½ cup at a time, stirring frequently. Wait until each addition is almost completely absorbed before adding the next ½ cup, reserving about ¼ cup to add at the end. Stir frequently to prevent sticking.

5. After approximately 18 minutes, when the rice is tender but still firm, turn off the heat and immediately add the reserved broth and the condimenti—cream, Parmesan, and parsley—and stir vigorously to combine with the rice. Serve immediately.

Serves 4

VARIATIONS

1. If you use unsweetened canned beets, add them in step 5 with the condimenti.

2. In Liguria, beet risotto is made with beet greens and fresh basil. Omit the diced fresh beets and add 1 cup chopped fresh beet greens, washed, from 2 to 3 beets, with ¼ cup light cream, ⅓ cup grated Parmesan cheese, and 2 tablespoons chopped fresh basil to the rice in step 5.

Pumpkin

RISOTTO
CON LA ZUCCA

We make this risotto with either pumpkin or butternut squash; both produce a pale orange and unusually sweet risotto. To show off the high color and complement the taste, this risotto is best when served in tandem with one of the piquant green risotti, such as spinach (see page 39). When this risotto is made into croquettes (see page 314) it is a delicious side dish for an entrée of roast turkey or duck.

CONDIMENTI	¼ pound fresh or frozen pumpkin or butternut squash, or 1 cup canned unsweetened pumpkin purée
	1 tablespoon lemon juice
	1 tablespoon chopped fresh parsley
	1 tablespoon unsalted butter
	¼ cup grated Parmesan cheese
BRODO	5½ cups Basic Broth (see page 14), approximately
SOFFRITTO	2 tablespoons unsalted butter
	1 tablespoon oil
	⅓ cup finely minced onion
RISO	1½ cups Arborio rice

1. *CONDIMENTI:* If you are using fresh pumpkin or squash, peel, remove seeds, and cut into 1-inch pieces. Cook fresh or frozen pumpkin or squash with 1 cup water until it is tender and can easily be pierced with a fork, about 15 minutes. Place pumpkin with ½ cup of its cooking liquid in a food processor, blender, or food mill and purée. Set aside. (If you are using canned pumpkin, omit this step.)

2. *BRODO:* Bring the broth to a steady simmer in a saucepan on top of the stove.

3. *SOFFRITTO:* Heat the butter and oil in a heavy 4-quart casserole over moderate heat. Add the onion and sauté for 1 to 2 minutes, until it begins to soften, being careful not to brown it.

4. *RISO:* Add the rice to the soffritto; using a wooden spoon, stir for 1 minute, making sure all the grains are well coated. Begin to add the simmering broth, ½ cup at a time, stirring frequently. Wait until each addition is almost completely absorbed before adding the next ½ cup, reserving about ¼ cup to add at the end. Stir frequently to prevent sticking.

5. After approximately 18 minutes, when the rice is tender but still firm, add the reserved broth and the condimenti—pumpkin or squash, lemon juice, and parsley. Turn off the heat and immediately add the butter and Parmesan and stir vigorously to combine with the rice. Serve immediately.

Serves 4

VARIATION

Add 1 cup finely shredded radicchio and a pinch of nutmeg to the rice after the first addition of broth in step 4.

Cabbage

RISOTTO
AL CAVOLO

James Beard, who loved cabbage, believed that cabbage was misunderstood and underappreciated because most people were taught to boil it in lots of water until it was limp and flavorless. Cooking cabbage in risotto, on the other hand, brings out its best characteristics and delicate flavor. Use curly-leaf Savoy cabbage if you can find it; it's the type most widely used in Italy.

BRODO	5 cups Basic Broth (see page 14), approximately
	½ cup dry white wine or broth
SOFFRITTO	2 tablespoons unsalted butter
	1 tablespoon oil
	⅓ cup finely minced onion
	3 tablespoons finely minced carrot
	3 tablespoons finely minced celery
	1 garlic clove, finely minced
RISO	1½ cups Arborio rice

CONDIMENTI   8 ounces cabbage, finely shredded (about 2 cups)

1 tablespoon tomato paste

1 tablespoon unsalted butter

⅓ cup grated Parmesan cheese

1 tablespoon chopped fresh parsley

1. BRODO: Bring the broth to a steady simmer in a saucepan on top of the stove.

2. SOFFRITTO: Heat the butter and oil in a heavy 4-quart casserole over moderate heat. Add the onion, carrot, celery, and garlic and sauté for 1 to 2 minutes, until the onion begins to soften, being careful not to brown it.

3. RISO: Add the rice to the soffritto; using a wooden spoon, stir for 1 minute, making sure all the grains are well coated. Add the wine and stir until it is completely absorbed.

4. CONDIMENTI: Add the cabbage and tomato paste and begin to add the simmering broth, ½ cup at a time, stirring frequently. Wait until each addition is almost completely absorbed before adding the next ½ cup, reserving about ¼ cup to add at the end. Stir frequently to prevent sticking.

5. After approximately 18 minutes, when the rice is tender but still firm, add the reserved broth. Turn off the heat and add the remaining condimenti—butter, Parmesan, and parsley—and stir vigorously to combine with the rice. Serve immediately.

Serves 4

VARIATIONS

1. For a heartier version, add 1 tablespoon finely chopped prosciutto to the soffritto.

2. To make the dish creamier, add 3 ounces mozzarella cheese with the butter and Parmesan cheese, or add 3 ounces Mascarpone in place of the butter.

NOTE: When choosing cabbage, the fresher and younger the better. Older cabbages, which tend toward bitterness, usually have their dark, tough outer leaves pruned away so all you see is a light green head. Younger cabbages will have their dark green leaves attached.

Beans

RISOTTO
CON FAGIOLI

Throughout most of Italy you find beans combined with pasta *(pasta e fagioli)*. Risotto con Fagioli is the Northern Italian version. The added tomatoes and herbs make this a savory and hearty dish.

BRODO	5 cups Basic Broth (see page 14), approximately
SOFFRITTO	2 tablespoons unsalted butter
	1 tablespoon oil
	⅓ cup finely minced onion
	1 small tomato peeled, seeded, and chopped, or ¼ cup canned Italian plum tomatoes, well drained and chopped
RISO	1½ cups Arborio rice

CONDIMENTI   1 cup canned cannellini beans, rinsed and drained (see Note)

1 tablespoon unsalted butter

⅓ cup grated Parmesan cheese

1 tablespoon chopped fresh parsley

1 tablespoon finely chopped fresh basil, or ¼ teaspoon dried

1. BRODO: Bring the broth to a steady simmer in a saucepan on top of the stove.

2. SOFFRITTO: Heat the butter and oil in a heavy 4-quart casserole over moderate heat. Add the onion and sauté for 1 to 2 minutes, until it begins to soften, being careful not to brown it. Add the tomato and cook for 3 to 5 minutes.

3. RISO: Add the rice to the soffritto; using a wooden spoon, stir for 1 minute, making sure all the grains are well coated. Add ½ cup broth and stir until it is completely absorbed. Continue to add the simmering broth, ½ cup at a time, stirring frequently. Wait until each addition is almost completely absorbed before adding the next ½ cup, reserving about ¼ cup to add at the end. Stir frequently to prevent sticking.

4. CONDIMENTI: After approximately 18 minutes, when the rice is tender but still firm, add the reserved broth. Turn off the heat and immediately add the condimenti—beans, butter, Parmesan, parsley, and basil—and stir vigorously to combine with the rice. Serve immediately.

Serves 4

NOTE: Cannellini beans are widely available in cans. If you want to use dried beans, we recommend the Great Northern or white kidney variety. For this recipe, use ½ cup beans. Place them in a heatproof bowl. Cover with boiling water, and soak them overnight. Drain. Place in a large saucepan with 5 cups water and 1 teaspoon salt, bring to a boil, and simmer for 1 hour, or until tender.

Country-Style I

RISOTTO
ALLA PAESANA

Throughout Northern Italy there are many variations of the rustic Risotto alla Paesana. This version, which comes from the area around Turin, is flavored with fresh tomatoes and acorn or butternut squash. Uncooked tender baby peas are added for their fresh taste and a colorful flourish of green. The heat from the rice cooks the peas just enough to leave them bright green and a bit crunchy.

BRODO	5½ cups Basic Broth (see page 14), approximately
SOFFRITTO	2 tablespoons unsalted butter
	1 tablespoon oil
	⅓ cup finely minced onion
CONDIMENTI	2 plum tomatoes, peeled, seeded, and chopped, or ½ cup canned Italian plum tomatoes, well drained and chopped
	2 cups grated acorn or butternut squash
	1 tablespoon unsalted butter
	⅓ cup grated Parmesan cheese
	½ cup fresh peas or defrosted frozen baby peas, not cooked
RISO	1½ cups Arborio rice

1. *BRODO:* Bring the broth to a steady simmer in a saucepan on top of the stove.

2. *SOFFRITTO:* Heat the butter and oil in a heavy 4-quart casserole over moderate heat. Add the onion and sauté for 1 to 2 minutes, until it begins to soften, being careful not to brown it.

3. *CONDIMENTI:* Add the tomatoes and squash and 1 cup of water to the soffritto, and cook for 10 minutes, until the water has evaporated and the squash is almost tender.

4. *RISO:* Add the rice to tomatoes and squash; using a wooden spoon, stir for 1 minute, making sure all the grains are well coated. Begin to add the simmering broth, ½ cup at a time, stirring frequently. Wait until each addition is almost completely absorbed before adding the next ½ cup, reserving about ¼ cup to add at the end. Stir frequently to prevent sticking.

5. After approximately 18 minutes, when the rice is tender but still firm, add the reserved broth. Turn off the heat and immediately add the remaining condimenti—butter, Parmesan, and peas—and stir vigorously to combine with the rice. Serve immediately.

Serves 4

Country-Style II

This country-style risotto is a hearty dish worthy of a chilly fall evening. Italians prepare this risotto by adding all of the vegetables to the pot before the rice. We have found, however, that this upsets the timing and the amount of liquid needed to cook the risotto, so we prefer to sauté the vegetables separately and add them at the end of the cooking process to get more of the individual flavors and textures of the vegetables.

CONDIMENTI	2 tablespoons olive oil
	1 garlic clove, finely minced
	2 small Italian plum tomatoes, peeled, seeded, and chopped, or ½ cup canned Italian tomatoes, well drained and chopped
	10 green beans, cut into ½-inch pieces
	1 small zucchini, about 4 ounces, washed, stem removed, diced
	¼ cup fresh peas or defrosted frozen baby peas, not cooked
	1 tablespoon unsalted butter
	⅓ cup grated Parmesan cheese
BRODO	5½ cups Basic Broth (see page 14), approximately

SOFFRITTO	2 tablespoons unsalted butter
	1 tablespoon oil
	⅓ cup finely minced onion
	3 tablespoons finely minced carrot
	3 tablespoons finely minced celery
	1 tablespoon chopped fresh parsley

RISO	1½ cups Arborio rice

1. CONDIMENTI: Heat the olive oil in a skillet over low heat; add the garlic, tomatoes, green beans, and zucchini, and gently sauté until zucchini and beans are barely tender, about 8 to 10 minutes. Turn off heat and set aside.

2. BRODO: Bring the broth to a steady simmer in a saucepan on top of the stove.

3. SOFFRITTO: Heat the butter and oil in a heavy 4-quart casserole over moderate heat. Add the onion, carrot, celery, and parsley, and sauté for 1 to 2 minutes, until the onion begins to soften, being careful not to brown it.

4. RISO: Add the rice to the soffritto; using a wooden spoon, stir for 1 minute, making sure all the grains are well coated. Begin to add the simmering broth, ½ cup at a time, stirring frequently. Wait until each addition is almost completely absorbed before adding the next ½ cup, reserving about ¼ cup to add at the end. Stir frequently to prevent sticking.

5. After approximately 18 minutes, when the rice is tender but still firm, add the reserved broth and the condimenti—the tomato-green beans-zucchini mixture and the peas. Turn off the heat, immediately add the butter and Parmesan, and stir vigorously to combine with the rice. Serve immediately.

Serves 4

Fresh Mushrooms

RISOTTO
AI FUNGHI

In Italy, fresh mushrooms are usually wild varieties with lots of character. In America, cultivated mushrooms with perfect white caps and little in the way of taste are the most widely available. For this risotto, we mix our mushrooms—equal parts cultivated and wild varieties, such as shiitake and oyster *(pleurotte),* or Portobello (also called Roman)—to bring out the most mushroom flavor. Serve with an aged Chianti Riserva and some *bruschetta,* grilled garlic bread.

CONDIMENTI	3 tablespoons unsalted butter
	4 ounces shiitake or other wild mushrooms, stems removed, sliced (about 2 cups)
	4 ounces cultivated white mushrooms, stems removed, sliced (about 1 cup)
	Salt and freshly ground black pepper
	¼ cup Mascarpone cheese or heavy cream
	¼ cup grated Parmesan cheese
	1 tablespoon chopped parsley
BRODO	5 cups Basic Broth (see page 14), approximately
	½ cup dry white wine or broth

SOFFRITTO	2 tablespoons unsalted butter
	1 tablespoon oil
	⅓ cup finely minced onion
RISO	1½ cups Arborio rice

1. CONDIMENTI: Heat the butter in a small skillet over moderate heat. When it begins to foam, add the mushrooms and cook for 3 to 5 minutes, until they are soft. Add salt and pepper to taste. Turn off the heat and set aside.

2. BRODO: Bring the broth to a steady simmer in a saucepan on top of the stove.

3. SOFFRITTO: Heat the butter and oil in a heavy 4-quart casserole over moderate heat. Add the onion and sauté for 1 to 2 minutes, until it begins to soften, being careful not to brown it.

4. RISO: Add the rice to the soffritto; using a wooden spoon, stir for 1 minute, making sure all the grains are well coated. Add the wine and stir until it is completely absorbed. Begin to add the simmering broth, ½ cup at a time, stirring frequently. Wait until each addition is almost completely absorbed before adding the next ½ cup, reserving about ¼ cup to add at the end. Stir frequently to prevent sticking.

5. After approximately 18 minutes, when the rice is tender but still firm, add the reserved broth and the condimenti—mushrooms, Mascarpone, Parmesan, and parsley—and stir vigorously until the cheeses are melted and combined with the rice. Serve immediately.

Serves 4

Fresh Mushrooms, Cognac, & Cream

RISOTTO
CON FUNGHI, COGNAC E PANNA

The trio of shiitake mushrooms, Cognac, and cream creates a symphony of flavors. You'll need a fine Cognac, or another good-quality brandy, to get the full effect. Serve this elegant dish as a first course before an entrée of pan-broiled fillet of beef.

CONDIMENTI	1 tablespoon unsalted butter
	4 ounces shiitake mushrooms, or 8 ounces white cultivated mushrooms, stems removed and sliced (about 2 cups)
	Salt and freshly ground black pepper
	½ cup Cognac or brandy
	½ cup light cream
	⅓ cup grated Parmesan cheese
	1 tablespoon chopped fresh parsley
BRODO	5 cups Basic Broth (see page 14), approximately
SOFFRITTO	2 tablespoons unsalted butter
	1 tablespoon oil
	½ cup finely minced shallots
RISO	1½ cups Arborio rice

1. CONDIMENTI: Heat the butter in a skillet over moderate heat. When it begins to foam, add the mushrooms and cook, stirring frequently, for 3 to 5 minutes, until the mushrooms are soft. Add salt and pepper to taste. Turn the heat to high, add the Cognac, and cook until it is reduced by half. Lower heat, add the cream, and continue cooking, for about 5 minutes longer, until the cream has reduced slightly and thickened. Turn off the heat and set aside.

2. BRODO: Bring the broth to a steady simmer in a saucepan on top of the stove.

3. SOFFRITTO: Heat the butter and oil in a heavy 4-quart casserole over moderate heat. Add the onion and sauté for 1 to 2 minutes, until it begins to soften, being careful not to brown it.

4. RISO: Add the rice to the soffritto; using a wooden spoon, stir for 1 minute, making sure all the grains are well coated. Begin to add the simmering broth, ½ cup at a time. Wait until each addition is almost completely absorbed before adding the next ½ cup. Stir frequently to prevent sticking.

5. After approximately 18 minutes, when the rice is tender but still firm, add the condimenti—the mushroom-Cognac-cream mixture, Parmesan, and parsley—and stir vigorously to combine with the rice. Serve immediately.

Serves 4

Mushrooms & Green Peppercorns

RISOTTO
CON FUNGHI E PEPE VERDE

This is an excellent way to get the most flavor from white cultivated mushrooms. Chopped fine and slowly simmered with the rice, the mushrooms' taste is transformed from the ordinary to the extraordinary. The green peppercorns add zest.

CONDIMENTI	3 tablespoons unsalted butter
	½ cup finely minced onion
	8 ounces white mushrooms, stems and caps, finely chopped (about 1½ cups)
	2 teaspoons green peppercorns, drained
	¼ cup heavy cream
	⅓ cup grated Parmesan cheese
BRODO	5 cups Basic Broth (see page 14), approximately
	½ cup dry Marsala or broth
SOFFRITTO	2 tablespoons unsalted butter
	1 tablespoon oil
	1 garlic clove, finely minced
	⅓ cup finely minced onion
RISO	1½ cups Arborio rice

1. CONDIMENTI: Heat the butter in a small skillet over moderate heat. Add the onion and cook for 3 to 5 minutes, until it turns golden. Add the mushrooms and green peppercorns and continue cooking for 5 minutes longer. Turn off the heat and set aside.

2. BRODO: Bring the broth to a steady simmer in a saucepan on top of the stove.

3. SOFFRITTO: Heat the butter and oil in a heavy 4-quart casserole over moderate heat. Add the onion and garlic and sauté for 1 to 2 minutes, until the onion begins to soften, being careful not to brown it.

4. RISO: Add the rice to the soffritto; using a wooden spoon, stir for 1 minute, making sure all the grains are well coated. Add the Marsala and stir until it is completely absorbed. Add the condimenti—mushrooms and green peppercorns—and begin to add the simmering broth, ½ cup at a time, stirring frequently. Wait until each addition is almost completely absorbed before adding the next ½ cup, reserving about ¼ cup to add at the end. Stir frequently to prevent sticking.

5. After approximately 18 minutes, when the rice is tender but still firm, add the reserved broth and the remaining condimenti—cream and Parmesan—and stir vigorously to combine with the rice. Serve immediately.

Serves 4

VARIATION

Substitute chopped shallots for the onion in the soffritto and ½ cup red wine for the Marsala.

Mushrooms & Tomatoes

RISOTTO
CON FUNGHI E POMODORI

The woodsy flavor of fresh wild mushrooms combines with the tomatoes to create a risotto with a rich earthy character. We like to serve this dish with a full-bodied red wine, such as a Vino Nobile di Montepulciano or a Chianti Classico, before an entrée of veal chops sautéed with fresh fennel and shallots.

CONDIMENTI	2 tablespoons unsalted butter
	4 ounces shiitake mushrooms, or 8 ounces white cultivated mushrooms, stems removed, sliced (about 2 cups)
	2 small tomatoes, peeled, seeded, and chopped, or ½ cup canned Italian tomatoes, well drained and chopped
	Salt and freshly ground black pepper
	⅓ cup grated Parmesan cheese
	1 tablespoon chopped fresh parsley
BRODO	5 cups Basic Broth (see page 14), approximately
	½ cup dry white wine or broth

SOFFRITTO	2 tablespoons unsalted butter
	1 tablespoon oil
	⅓ cup finely minced onion

RISO	1½ cups Arborio rice

1. CONDIMENTI: Heat the butter in a small skillet over moderate heat. When it begins to foam, add the mushrooms and tomatoes and gently sauté, stirring occasionally, for about 5 minutes, until the mushrooms are tender and the liquid from the tomatoes has almost evaporated. Add salt and pepper to taste. Turn off heat and set aside.

2. BRODO: Bring the broth to a steady simmer in a saucepan on top of the stove.

3. SOFFRITTO: Heat the butter and oil in a heavy 4-quart casserole over moderate heat. Add the onion and sauté for 1 to 2 minutes, until it begins to soften, being careful not to brown it.

4. RISO: Add the rice to the soffritto; using a wooden spoon, stir for 1 minute, making sure all the grains are well coated. Add the wine and stir until it is completely absorbed. Begin to add the simmering broth, ½ cup at a time, stirring frequently. Wait until each addition is almost completely absorbed before adding the next ½ cup, reserving about ¼ cup to add at the end. Stir frequently to prevent sticking.

5. After approximately 18 minutes, when the rice is tender but still firm, add the reserved broth and the condimenti—mushroom and tomato mixture, Parmesan, and parsley—and stir vigorously to combine with the rice. Serve immediately.

Serves 4

VARIATION

Add ¼ cup chopped prosciutto to the soffritto, and ½ cup fresh peas or defrosted frozen peas, not cooked, to the finished risotto in place of the parsley.

Mushrooms & Sausage

RISOTTO
CON FUNGHI E SALSICCIA

Fresh white cultivated mushrooms take center stage in this risotto, while the sausage and red wine serve as background flavoring. This ensemble produces a dish with a deliciously hearty and satisfying character. Serve before an entrée of braised eggplant cooked with tomatoes and sage.

CONDIMENTI	2 tablespoons unsalted butter
	12 ounces white cultivated mushrooms, stems removed, sliced (about 3 cups)
	½ cup light red wine, such as Bardolino or Valpolicella
	¼ cup grated Parmesan cheese
	1 tablespoon chopped fresh parsley
BRODO	5½ cups Basic Broth (see page 14), approximately
SOFFRITTO	2 tablespoons unsalted butter
	1 tablespoon oil
	3 tablespoons finely minced onion
	2 tablespoons minced carrot
	2 tablespoons minced celery
	3 ounces Italian sausage, casing removed (about 1 average-size sausage)
RISO	1½ cups Arborio rice

1. CONDIMENTI: Heat the butter in a skillet over moderate heat. When it begins to foam, add the mushrooms and continue cooking for 3 to 5 minutes, until they are soft. Add the red wine, turn the heat to high, and boil vigorously until the liquid is almost completely evaporated. Turn off heat and set aside.

2. BRODO: Bring the broth to a steady simmer in a saucepan on top of the stove.

3. SOFFRITTO: Heat the butter and oil in a heavy 4-quart casserole over moderate heat. Add the onion, carrot, and celery and sauté for 1 to 2 minutes, until the onion begins to soften, being careful not to brown it. Add the sausage; using a fork, break up the meat while stirring, until it loses its pink color and begins to brown.

4. RISO: Add the rice to the soffritto; using a wooden spoon, stir for 1 minute, making sure all the grains are well coated. Begin to add the simmering broth, ½ cup at a time, stirring frequently. Wait until each addition is almost completely absorbed before adding the next ½ cup, reserving about ¼ cup to add at the end. Stir frequently to prevent sticking.

5. After approximately 18 minutes, when the rice is tender but still firm, add the reserved broth and the condimenti—mushrooms, Parmesan, and parsley—and stir vigorously to combine with the rice. Serve immediately.

Serves 4

Fresh Mushrooms & Dried Porcini

Bosco is the Italian word for forest. This risotto captures the essence of the woodsy taste of the fresh wild mushrooms and dried porcini. Serve this risotto as a first course before an entrée of veal or highly seasoned grilled scampi, or as a main course preceded by a salad of sliced tomatoes and mozzarella topped with fresh basil and extra-virgin olive oil.

CONDIMENTI	⅓-ounce package dried porcini, approximately
	2 tablespoons unsalted butter
	4 ounces shiitake or other wild mushrooms, stems removed and sliced (about 2 cups), or 8 ounces white cultivated mushrooms, stems removed and sliced
	¼ cup light cream
	Salt and freshly ground black pepper
	⅓ cup grated Parmesan cheese
	1 tablespoon chopped fresh parsley
BRODO	4 cups Basic Broth (see page 14), approximately
	1 cup porcini liquid, strained
	½ cup dry white wine or broth

SOFFRITTO	2 tablespoons unsalted butter
	1 tablespoon oil
	⅓ cup finely minced onion

RISO	1½ cups Arborio rice

1. CONDIMENTI: Place the porcini in a small bowl with 1 cup boiling or very hot water and let stand for 30 minutes. Strain the porcini liquid into a saucepan with the broth. Heat the butter in a small skillet over moderate heat. When it begins to foam, add the fresh mushrooms and cook, stirring for 3 to 5 minutes, until the mushrooms are soft and the liquid they give off has almost completely evaporated. Coarsely chop the porcini and add them to the pan with the fresh mushrooms. Continue cooking for about 2 minutes longer. Add the cream and simmer until it is reduced slightly and thickened. Add salt and pepper to taste. Turn off the heat and set aside.

2. BRODO: Bring the broth, combined with the liquid from the porcini, to a steady simmer in a saucepan on top of the stove.

3. SOFFRITTO: Heat the butter and oil in a heavy 4-quart casserole over moderate heat. Add the onion and sauté for 1 to 2 minutes, until it begins to soften, being careful not to brown it.

4. RISO: Add the rice to the soffritto; using a wooden spoon, stir for 1 minute, making sure all the grains are well coated. Add the wine and stir until it is completely absorbed. Begin to add the simmering broth, ½ cup at a time, stirring frequently. Wait until each addition is almost completely absorbed before adding the next ½ cup, reserving about ¼ cup to add at the end. Stir frequently to prevent sticking.

5. After approximately 18 minutes, when the rice is tender but still firm, add the reserved broth and the condimenti—mushrooms and cream, Parmesan, and parsley—and stir vigorously to combine with the rice. Serve immediately.

Serves 4

Porcini & Prosciutto

RISOTTO
ALLA CASTELLANA

This risotto calls for a good domestic or imported Italian prosciutto; finely chopped, it yields more flavor. Use fresh tomatoes if you have them on hand. This makes a great main course served with steamed green beans and broccoli quickly sautéed in olive oil.

CONDIMENTI	¾-ounce package dried porcini, approximately
	1 tablespoon unsalted butter
	¼ cup grated Parmesan cheese
	1 tablespoon chopped fresh parsley
BRODO	4 cups Basic Broth (see page 14), approximately
	1 cup porcini liquid, strained
	½ cup dry white wine or broth
SOFFRITTO	2 tablespoons unsalted butter
	1 tablespoon oil
	⅓ cup finely minced onion
	¼ cup finely chopped prosciutto
	2 small tomatoes, peeled, seeded, and chopped, or ½ cup canned Italian tomatoes, well drained and chopped
RISO	1½ cups Arborio rice

1. CONDIMENTI: Put the porcini in a small bowl with 1 cup boiling or very hot water and allow to stand for 30 minutes. Strain the liquid into a saucepan with the broth. Chop the porcini and set aside.

2. BRODO: Bring the broth, combined with the liquid from the porcini, to a steady simmer in a saucepan on top of the stove.

3. SOFFRITTO: Heat the butter and oil in a heavy 4-quart casserole over moderate heat. Add the onion, prosciutto, and tomatoes, and sauté for 1 to 2 minutes, until the onion begins to soften, being careful not to brown it.

4. RISO: Add the rice to the soffritto; using a wooden spoon, stir for 1 minute, making sure all the grains are well coated. Add the porcini. Pour in the wine and stir until it is completely absorbed. Begin to add the simmering broth, ½ cup at a time, stirring frequently. Wait until each addition is almost completely absorbed before adding the next ½ cup, reserving about ¼ cup to add at the end. Stir frequently to prevent sticking.

5. After approximately 18 minutes, when the rice is tender but still firm, add the reserved broth. Turn off the heat and add the remaining condimenti—butter, Parmesan, and parsley—and stir vigorously to combine with the rice. Serve immediately.

Serves 4

Porcini, Veal, & Sage

RISOTTO
CON PORCINI, VITELLO E SALVIA

This is a hearty main-course risotto made with dried porcini and ground
veal, with a touch of fresh tomato and sage. Precede it with a warm salad
of steamed fresh spinach and lightly cooked beets in a tart red-wine and
olive-oil dressing.

CONDIMENTI	⅓-ounce package dried porcini, approximately
	1 tablespoon unsalted butter
	1 tablespoon minced fresh sage, or 1 teaspoon dried
	1 tablespoon chopped fresh parsley
	⅓ cup grated Parmesan cheese
BRODO	4 cups Basic Broth (see page 14), approximately
	1 cup porcini liquid, strained
	½ cup dry white wine or broth
SOFFRITTO	2 tablespoons unsalted butter
	1 tablespoon oil

⅓ cup finely minced onion

3 to 4 ounces lean veal, ground

1 small tomato, peeled, seeded, and chopped,
    or ¼ cup canned Italian tomatoes, well
    drained and chopped

Salt and freshly ground black pepper

RISO 1½ cups Arborio rice

1. CONDIMENTI: Place the porcini in a small bowl with 1 cup boiling or very hot water and allow to stand for 30 minutes. Strain the liquid into a saucepan with the broth. Chop the porcini coarsely and set aside.

2. BRODO: Bring the broth, combined with the porcini liquid, to a steady simmer in a saucepan on top of the stove.

3. SOFFRITTO: Heat the butter and oil in a heavy 4-quart casserole over moderate heat. Add the onion and sauté until it begins to soften. Add the veal and tomato; using a fork, stir the veal for 3 to 5 minutes, until it loses its pink color, being careful not to brown it. Add salt and pepper to taste.

4. RISO: Add the rice to the soffritto; using a wooden spoon, stir for 1 minute, making sure all the grains are well coated. Add the porcini. Pour in the wine and stir until it is completely absorbed. Begin to add the simmering broth, ½ cup at a time, stirring frequently. Wait until each addition is almost completely absorbed before adding the next ½ cup, reserving about ¼ cup to add at the end. Stir frequently to prevent sticking.

5. After approximately 18 minutes, when the rice is tender but still firm, add the reserved broth and remaining condimenti—butter, sage, parsley, and Parmesan—and stir vigorously to combine with the rice. Serve immediately.

Serves 4

Porcini & Arugula

RISOTTO
CON PORCINI E RUCOLA

Arugula, with its peppery taste, is a customary salad green in Italy. We found that it adds a nice contrast to this rich risotto of porcini and Fontina. It is a hearty first course which complements a savory roasted leg of lamb.

CONDIMENTI	⅓-ounce package dried porcini, approximately
	1 small bunch of arugula, chopped (about 1 cup)
	2 ounces Italian Fontina cheese, rind removed, cut into small pieces
	¼ cup grated Parmesan cheese
BRODO	4 cups Basic Broth (see page 14), approximately
	1 cup porcini liquid, strained
	½ cup dry white wine or broth
SOFFRITTO	2 tablespoons unsalted butter
	1 tablespoon oil
	⅓ cup finely mined onion
RISO	1½ cups Arborio rice

1. CONDIMENTI: Place the porcini in a small bowl with 1 cup boiling or very hot water and let stand for 30 minutes. Strain the liquid into a saucepan with the broth. Chop the porcini and set aside.

2. BRODO: Bring the broth combined with the porcini liquid to a steady simmer in a saucepan on top of the stove.

3. SOFFRITTO: Heat the butter and oil in a heavy 4-quart casserole over moderate heat. Add the onion and sauté for 1 to 2 minutes, until it begins to soften, being careful not to brown it.

4. RISO: Add the rice to the soffritto; using a wooden spoon, stir for 1 minute, making sure all the grains are well coated. Add the porcini. Pour in the wine and stir until it is completely absorbed. Begin to add the simmering broth, ½ cup at a time. Wait until each addition is almost completely absorbed before adding the next ½ cup, reserving about ¼ cup to add at the end. Stir frequently to prevent sticking.

5. After approximately 18 minutes, when the rice is tender but still firm, add the reserved broth and the remaining condimenti—arugula, Fontina, and Parmesan—and stir vigorously until the cheeses are melted and combined with the rice. Serve immediately.

Serves 4

Dried Porcini, Spinach, & Peas

RISOTTO
CON PORCINI E VERDURE

Dried porcini, spinach, and tender sweet peas provide a great combination of tastes and textures. This risotto makes a light but satisfying main course; or serve it as a first course before game or meat.

CONDIMENTI	¾-ounce package dried porcini, approximately
	1 tablespoon olive oil
	1 garlic clove, finely minced
	1 tablespoon chopped fresh parsley
	1 cup packed fresh spinach leaves, washed, stems removed, and coarsely chopped
	½ cup fresh peas or defrosted frozen baby peas, not cooked
	¼ cup light cream
	⅓ cup grated Parmesan cheese
BRODO	4 cups Basic Broth (see page 14), approximately
	1 cup porcini liquid, strained
	½ cup dry white wine or broth

SOFFRITTO	2 tablespoons unsalted butter
	1 tablespoon oil
	2 tablespoons finely minced onion
RISO	1½ cups Arborio rice

1. CONDIMENTI: Place the porcini in a small bowl with 1 cup boiling or very hot water and allow to stand for 30 minutes. Strain the liquid into a saucepan with the broth. Chop the porcini. Heat the oil and garlic in a skillet over moderate heat. Add porcini and cook for 2 minutes to heat the mushrooms through. Add the parsley; stir to combine. Turn off the heat and set aside.

2. BRODO: Bring the broth and the strained porcini liquid to a steady simmer in a saucepan on top of the stove.

3. SOFFRITTO: Heat the butter and oil in a heavy 4-quart casserole over moderate heat. Add the onion and sauté for 1 to 2 minutes, until it begins to soften, being careful not to brown it.

4. RISO: Add the rice to the soffritto; using a wooden spoon, stir for 1 minute, making sure all the grains are well coated. Add the wine and stir until it is completely absorbed. Begin to add the simmering broth, ½ cup at a time, stirring frequently. Wait until each addition is almost completely absorbed before adding the next ½ cup, reserving about ¼ cup to add at the end. Stir frequently to prevent sticking.

5. Add the porcini and parsley mixture and the spinach after the rice has been cooking for 10 minutes. Continue to add the broth, ½ cup at a time. After approximately 18 minutes, when the rice is tender but still firm, add the reserved broth and the remaining condimenti—peas, cream, and Parmesan—and stir vigorously to combine with the rice. Serve immediately.

Serves 4

White Truffle

RISOTTO
AL TARTUFO BIANCO

The white truffle is one of Italy's most prized specialties. Grown primarily near Alba in Piedmont, it has a unique earthy flavor and fragrance that make it an extraordinary culinary delight; it is almost always eaten raw. Fresh white truffles are in season and available for only a short time in the late fall, which is when you should prepare this risotto. (Canned white truffles are available all year; we don't recommend them, as their flavor has little in common with the fresh truffles.) There are special tools just for shaving truffles, but you can accomplish the task easily with a standard 4-sided kitchen grater if you use the single-blade grater on the side. You want the truffle cut paper-thin, so be careful to press down on the truffle with just a little pressure; too much force, and the shavings will be too thick.

BRODO	5 cups Basic Broth (see page 14), approximately
	½ cup dry white wine
SOFFRITTO	2 tablespoons unsalted butter
	1 tablespoon oil
	3 tablespoons finely minced onion
RISO	1½ cups Arborio rice
CONDIMENTI	¼ cup light cream
	⅓ cup grated Parmesan cheese
	1 fresh white truffle, shaved paper-thin

1. BRODO: Bring the broth to a steady simmer in a saucepan on top of the stove.

2. SOFFRITTO: Heat the butter and oil in a heavy 4-quart casserole over moderate heat. Add the onion and sauté for 1 to 2 minutes, until it begins to soften, being careful not to brown it.

3. RISO: Add the rice to the soffritto; using a wooden spoon, stir for 1 minute, making sure all the grains are well coated. Add the wine and stir until it is completely absorbed. Begin to add the simmering broth, ½ cup at a time, stirring frequently. Wait until each addition is almost completely absorbed before adding the next ½ cup, reserving about ¼ cup to add at the end. Stir frequently to prevent sticking.

4. CONDIMENTI: After approximately 18 minutes, when the rice is tender but still firm, add the reserved broth and the condimenti—cream and Parmesan—and stir vigorously to combine with the rice. Garnish each serving with truffle shavings. Serve immediately.

Serves 4

Black Truffle

Black truffles are found in the region around Norcia in Umbria. Their delicate, almost nutty flavor is different from either the pungent-tasting white truffles from Alba or the intensely rich French black truffles from Périgord. Unlike white truffles, which are almost always added as a garnish to risotto, in this dish the truffle is stirred into a just-finished risotto. The hot rice has the perfect temperature to bring out the unique earthy taste of the black truffle.

BRODO	5½ cups Basic Broth (see page 14), approximately
SOFFRITTO	3 tablespoons unsalted butter
RISO	1½ cups Arborio rice
CONDIMENTI	1 tablespoon unsalted butter
	¼ cup light cream
	⅓ cup grated Parmesan cheese
	1 black truffle, about 3½ ounces, fresh or preserved, coarsely minced

1. BRODO: Bring the broth to a steady simmer in a saucepan on top of the stove.

2. SOFFRITTO: Heat the butter in a heavy 4-quart casserole over moderate heat, being careful not to brown it.

3. *RISO:* Add the rice to the soffritto; using a wooden spoon, stir for 1 minute, making sure all the grains are well coated. Begin to add the simmering broth, ½ cup at a time, stirring frequently. Wait until each addition is almost completely absorbed before adding the next ½ cup, reserving about ¼ cup to add at the end. Stir frequently to prevent sticking.

4. *CONDIMENTI:* While the rice is cooking, melt the butter with the cream in a small saucepan and set aside. After approximately 18 minutes, when the rice is tender but still firm, add the reserved broth. Turn off the heat and add the condimenti—the butter and cream mixture, Parmesan, and black truffle—and stir vigorously to combine with the rice. Serve immediately.

Serves 4

VARIATION

Add ¼ teaspoon powdered saffron to the rice in step 3.

Fish & Seafood Risotti

THERE is no better way to enjoy the treasures the sea has to offer than in risotti made with fresh fish and shellfish. They bring out, complement, and enhance every bit of the taste of these seagoing delicacies. The rice creates a rich and creamy medium through which the flavors emerge. At the same time, the gentle textures of both the rice and fish come together so that each wonderful bite is harmony on the palate.

These risotti are different from most others in this book in one important respect: The hearty meat broth called for in all of the other risotti in this book is usually replaced with a flavorful fish broth (see page 17) or broth made from shellfish. Another distinction is that many of these risotti are made without the addition of Parmesan cheese, because its robust flavor can overpower the delicate taste of some fish and shellfish.

We are certain that this treasure trove of risotti will open up for you a whole new way of enjoying fish and seafood.

Fish Risotti

Cod, Yellow Pepper, & Capers

RISOTTO
CON MERLUZZO E PEPERONI

Cod, or *merluzzo,* is plentiful in Italy and lends itself to many risotto preparations. We adapted this risotto from a recipe created by Boston chef Betsy West. The peppers and capers add a zesty touch to the cod, which is added at the very end so that it doesn't overcook. Serve this as a main course for lunch or dinner after an *antipasto* of steamed broccoli and cauliflower in a pesto dressing.

BRODO	5 cups Basic Fish Broth (see page 17), approximately
	½ cup dry white wine or broth
SOFFRITTO	2 tablespoons unsalted butter
	1 tablespoon oil
	⅓ cup finely minced onion
	½ cup diced yellow pepper
RISO	1½ cups Arborio rice
CONDIMENTI	½ pound boneless cod, scrod, or pollack, cut into 1-inch pieces
	¼ cup light cream

⅓ cup grated Parmesan cheese

¼ cup chopped fresh parsley

1 tablespoon capers

1. BRODO: Bring the broth to a steady simmer in a saucepan on top of the stove.

2. SOFFRITTO: Heat the butter and oil in a heavy 4-quart casserole over moderate heat. Add the onion and diced pepper and sauté for 1 to 2 minutes, until the onion begins to soften, being careful not to brown it.

3. RISO: Add the rice to the soffritto; using a wooden spoon, stir for 1 minute, making sure all the grains are well coated. Add the wine and stir until it is completely absorbed. Begin to add the simmering broth, ½ cup at a time, stirring frequently. Wait until each addition is almost completely absorbed before adding the next ½ cup, reserving about ¼ cup to add at the end. Stir frequently to prevent sticking.

4. CONDIMENTI: After approximately 18 minutes, when the rice is tender but still firm, add the reserved broth and the condimenti—cod, cream, Parmesan, parsley, and capers—and stir vigorously to combine with the rice. Serve immediately.

Serves 4

VARIATIONS

1. Substitute sweet red bell pepper for the yellow pepper.
2. Use finely minced green Spanish olives in place of the capers.

Salt Cod

RISOTTO
CON BACCALÀ ALLA VICENTINA

Cod remains one of the world's most abundant and versatile fish, and *baccalà,* salt-preserved cod fillets, has been a staple food in Italy for centuries. It is a specialty of Vicenza, a city that lies between Verona and Venice, where risotto is prepared *alla vicentina,* with preserved cod fillets that are cooked slowly with milk, then added to the finished risotto. Salting doesn't adversely affect either the taste or the texture of the fish, and in fact some people contend that it actually improves the flavor. However, it makes this one of the few risotti that requires some planning, since the cod must be soaked for at least 24 hours before you use it.

CONDIMENTI	4 ounces salt cod
	1 tablespoon unsalted butter
	1 tablespoon finely minced onion
	1 garlic clove, finely minced
	½ cup whole milk
	1 tablespoon chopped fresh parsley
	⅓ cup grated Parmesan cheese
BRODO	5½ cups Basic Fish Broth (see page 17), approximately
SOFFRITTO	2 tablespoons unsalted butter
	1 tablespoon oil
	⅓ cup finely minced onion

RISO   1½ cups Arborio rice

1. CONDIMENTI: The day before you plan to prepare the risotto, place the salt cod in a large bowl and cover with cold water; allow it to soak for 24 hours, changing the water once, if possible. Drain the fish, dry on paper towels, and cut it into 1-inch pieces. Heat the butter in a skillet over moderate heat; add the onion and garlic and cook for 1 to 2 minutes, until the onion begins to soften. Add the cod and stir to combine it with the onion. Pour in the milk and cook for 10 to 15 minutes, until the fish flakes easily with a fork and the milk has been reduced to about half. Use a fork to break the fish into small pieces and set aside.

2. BRODO: Bring the broth to a steady simmer in a saucepan on top of the stove.

3. SOFFRITTO: Heat the butter and oil in a heavy 4-quart casserole over moderate heat. Add the onion and sauté for 1 to 2 minutes, until it begins to soften, being careful not to brown it.

4. RISO: Add the rice to the soffritto; using a wooden spoon, stir for 1 minute, making sure all the grains are well coated. Begin to add the simmering broth, ½ cup at a time, stirring frequently. Wait until each addition is almost completely absorbed before adding the next ½ cup, reserving about ¼ cup to add at the end. Stir frequently to prevent sticking.

5. After approximately 18 minutes, when the rice is tender but still firm, add the reserved broth and the condimenti—the cod and milk mixture, parsley, and Parmesan—and stir vigorously to combine with the rice. Serve immediately.

Serves 4

VARIATION

Soak the salt cod as directed and cut it into small uniform pieces. Heat 1 tablespoon olive oil in a skillet over moderate heat. Add 2 tablespoons minced onion, ½ cup chopped tomato (2 small tomatoes, peeled, seeded, and chopped), and the salt cod, and cook, stirring, for 5 to 8 minutes. Prepare the risotto as directed. Add the cod and tomatoes to the finished risotto with 1 tablespoon unsalted butter, ¼ cup grated Parmesan cheese, and 1 tablespoon chopped fresh parsley, and stir vigorously to combine with the rice. Serve immediately.

Perch

RISOTTO
CON IL PESCE PERSICO

A frequent offering of the trattorias in the small towns around Lake Como where perch is plentiful, this risotto is served at the table topped with fried perch filets. If freshwater perch are not available, you can substitute lake trout or ocean perch (also called redfish), flounder, or sea bass. Serve as a main course, followed by a green salad of Boston lettuce garnished with asparagus tips in a red-wine vinaigrette.

CONDIMENTI	4 to 6 fish fillets—perch, flounder, ocean perch
	1 whole egg, lightly beaten with 1 table-spoon water
	1 cup all-purpose flour
	5 tablespoons unsalted butter
	3 leaves of fresh sage, chopped, or 1 tea-spoon dried

BRODO	5 cups Basic Fish Broth (see page 17), approximately
	½ cup dry white wine or broth
SOFFRITTO	2 tablespoons unsalted butter
	1 tablespoon oil
	⅓ cup finely minced onion
	3 tablespoons finely minced carrot
	3 tablespoons finely minced celery
RISO	1½ cups Arborio rice

1. CONDIMENTI: Prepare the fish: dip each fish fillet into the egg and water mixture; dredge with flour, making sure the fillet is completely covered. Set on wax paper. Heat 2 tablespoons of the butter and the sage in a skillet over moderate heat. When the butter begins to foam, add 2 fish fillets. Brown the fillets on both sides (they will cook very quickly) and remove to a warm heatproof serving platter. Continue to add more butter and fillets until all are cooked. Place platter in a warm oven.

2. BRODO: Bring the broth to a steady simmer in a saucepan on top of the stove.

3. SOFFRITTO: Heat the butter and oil in a heavy 4-quart casserole over moderate heat. Add the onion, carrot, and celery and sauté for 1 to 2 minutes, until the onion begins to soften, being careful not to brown it.

4. RISO: Add the rice to the soffritto; using a wooden spoon, stir for 1 minute, making sure all the grains are well coated. Add the wine and stir until it is completely absorbed. Begin to add the simmering broth, ½ cup at a time, stirring frequently. Wait until each addition is almost completely absorbed before adding the next ½ cup, reserving about ¼ cup to add at the end. Stir frequently to prevent sticking.

5. After approximately 18 minutes, when the rice is tender but still firm, add the reserved broth. Turn off the heat and immediately add remaining tablespoon of butter, and stir vigorously to combine with the rice. Serve immediately, with 1 or 2 cooked fish fillets on each serving.

Serves 4

Monkfish in Tomato Basil Cream

RISOTTO
CON PESCE AL BASILICO

Monkfish, which also goes by the name of anglerfish, or *lotte* as it is called in France, is a firm-fleshed Atlantic Ocean fish, which derives its flavor from the lobster on which it feeds. Our favorite way to prepare it is with a rich cream sauce that's been delicately flavored with fresh tomatoes and basil, a preparation that lends itself perfectly to risotto. If monkfish is not available, use any firm-fleshed white fish, such as cusk, wolffish, halibut, or scrod. Serve this as a main course with simple accompaniments such as sautéed zucchini or a salad of radicchio and arugula.

CONDIMENTI	8 ounces monkfish, or any other firm white-fleshed fish, such as halibut or wolffish
	1 cup light cream
	1 small tomato, peeled, seeded, and chopped, or ¼ cup canned Italian tomatoes, well drained and chopped
	2 tablespoons finely chopped fresh basil
	Salt and freshly ground black pepper
BRODO	5 cups Basic Fish Broth (see page 17)
	½ cup dry white wine
SOFFRITTO	2 tablespoons unsalted butter
	1 tablespoon oil
	⅓ cup finely minced onion
RISO	1½ cups Arborio rice

1. CONDIMENTI: Place the fish in a small saucepan with 1 cup of fish broth. Cover and simmer for 10 to 12 minutes until it flakes easily with a fork. While fish is poaching, pour the cream into a skillet over moderate heat and simmer until it is reduced to about half. Stir in the tomato and basil and cook for 2 to 3 minutes longer, until the cream turns pink and the flavors meld. Drain the fish and strain the poaching liquid into a saucepan with the remaining broth. Cut fish into small pieces and add to the cream, tomato, and basil sauce. Add salt and pepper to taste. Set aside.

2. BRODO: Bring the broth to a steady simmer in a saucepan on top of the stove.

3. SOFFRITTO: Heat the butter and oil in a heavy 4-quart casserole over moderate heat. Add the onion and sauté for 1 to 2 minutes, until it begins to soften, being careful not to brown it.

4. RISO: Add the rice to the soffritto; using a wooden spoon, stir for 1 minute, making sure all the grains are well coated. Add the wine and stir until it is completely absorbed. Begin to add the simmering broth, ½ cup at a time, stirring frequently. Wait until each addition is almost completely absorbed before adding the next ½ cup. Stir frequently to prevent sticking.

5. After approximately 18 minutes, when the rice is tender but still firm, add the condimenti—the fish and cream sauce—and stir vigorously to combine with the rice. Serve immediately.

Serves 4

Salmon

RISOTTO
AL SALMONE

Chopped crisp watercress and fresh lemon juice enhance the delicate flavor of the salmon while the addition of sweet cream makes this dish rich, delicious, and heavenly. The raw salmon is cut into small pieces and added directly to the risotto, and it cooks in moments. Serve this risotto as a second course after a salad of yellow summer squash and sweet red pepper in a lemony dressing.

BRODO	5 cups Basic Fish Broth (see page 17), approximately
	½ cup dry white wine or broth

SOFFRITTO	2 tablespoons unsalted butter
	1 tablespoon oil
	⅓ cup finely minced onion

RISO	1½ cups Arborio rice

CONDIMENTI	6 ounces fresh salmon, fillet or steak, bones and skin removed, cut into slivers
	1 small bunch of watercress, washed and finely chopped (about 1 cup)
	2 tablespoons fresh lemon juice
	½ cup light cream
	1 tablespoon snipped fresh chives or chopped scallion greens

1. BRODO: Bring the broth to a steady simmer in a saucepan on top of the stove.

2. SOFFRITTO: Heat the butter and oil in a heavy 4-quart casserole over moderate heat. Add the onion and sauté for 1 to 2 minutes,

until it begins to soften, being careful not to brown it.

3. RISO: Add the rice to the soffritto; using a wooden spoon, stir for 1 minute, making sure all the grains are well coated. Add the wine and stir until it is completely absorbed. Begin to add the simmering broth, ½ cup at a time, stirring frequently. Wait until each addition is almost completely absorbed before adding the next ½ cup. Stir frequently to prevent sticking.

4. CONDIMENTI: After approximately 18 minutes, when the rice is tender but still firm, add the condimenti—salmon, watercress, lemon juice, cream, and chives—and stir vigorously to combine with the rice. Serve immediately.

Serves 4

Smoked Salmon

RISOTTO
AL SALMONE AFFUMICATO

This is an excellent brunch risotto, when served with crusty bread and Mascarpone cheese. For best results, use delicately flavored Norwegian, Scotch, or Irish smoked salmon and garnish each serving with a wedge of fresh lemon. Serve with sparkling dry white wine mixed with fresh orange juice.

BRODO	5 cups Basic Fish Broth (see page 17), approximately
	½ cup dry white wine or broth

SOFFRITTO	2 tablespoons unsalted butter
	1 tablespoon oil
	⅓ cup finely minced onion
RISO	1½ cups Arborio rice
CONDIMENTI	4 to 6 ounces smoked salmon, cut into thin strips, about ½ cup packed (see Note)
	Juice from 1 lemon, about ¼ cup
	½ cup light cream
	1 tablespoon chopped fresh parsley or fresh dill (do not use dried dill)
	1 whole lemon, cut into 4 wedges

1. BRODO: Bring the broth to a steady simmer in a saucepan on top of the stove.

2. SOFFRITTO: Heat the butter and oil in a heavy 4-quart casserole over moderate heat. Add the onion and sauté for 1 to 2 minutes, until it begins to soften, being careful not to brown it.

3. RISO: Add the rice to the soffritto; using a wooden spoon, stir for 1 to 2 minutes, making sure all the grains are well coated. Add the wine and stir until it is completely absorbed. Begin to add the simmering broth, ½ cup at a time, stirring frequently. Wait until each addition is almost completely absorbed before adding the next ½ cup. Stir frequently to prevent sticking.

4. CONDIMENTI: After approximately 18 minutes, when the rice is tender but still firm, add the condimenti—salmon, lemon juice, cream, and parsley—and stir vigorously to combine with the rice. Serve immediately with a wedge of lemon on each serving.

Serves 4

NOTE: If you can't obtain Norwegian or Scotch smoked salmon, you can use the saltier Nova salmon. However, because it is salty, marinate it in the lemon juice while you are preparing the risotto and decrease the quantity of salmon to 3 ounces.

VARIATION

A version we enjoyed in Brescia omitted the cream from step 4 and added 3 tablespoons of whiskey.

Swordfish

RISOTTO
CON IL PESCE SPADA

This risotto stands out as one of the few fish risotti in which the fish is served along with and not mixed into the rice; the freshest swordfish is marinated in vinegar and sautéed with mushrooms, tomato, and thyme to create a pungent fish ragoût, which is spooned over each serving of a saffron-flavored risotto. This makes a perfect summer dinner when swordfish is plentiful.

CONDIMENTI	4 to 6 ounces fresh swordfish steak, skin removed, cut into 1-inch pieces
	½ cup wine vinegar
	2 tablespoons unsalted butter
	1 tablespoon olive oil
	1 tablespoon finely minced onion
	1 tablespoon finely minced carrot
	1 tablespoon finely minced celery
	Pinch of dried thyme
	1 small fresh tomato, peeled, seeded, and chopped
	4 ounces mushrooms, sliced (1 cup)
	½ cup dry white wine
	Salt and freshly ground black pepper
	1 tablespoon chopped fresh parsley, for garnish
BRODO	5½ cups Basic Fish Broth (see page 17), approximately
	¼ teaspoon powdered saffron
SOFFRITTO	2 tablespoons unsalted butter
	1 tablespoon olive oil
	⅓ cup finely minced onion
RISO	1½ cups Arborio rice

1. CONDIMENTI: Place the fish pieces in a nonaluminum bowl with the vinegar and let stand for 10 minutes. Drain the fish and discard vinegar. Meanwhile, heat the butter and olive oil in a skillet over moderate heat with the onion, carrot, celery, and thyme, and cook for 2 to 3 minutes, until the onion begins to soften. Add the tomato and mushrooms and continue cooking for 3 to 5 minutes longer, until the mushrooms are tender. Add the fish and the wine, turn the heat to low, and simmer for about 10 minutes, until the wine has been reduced to a few tablespoons and the fish is cooked through. Add salt and pepper to taste. While the fish is cooking, prepare the risotto.

2. BRODO: Bring the broth with the saffron to a steady simmer in a saucepan on top of the stove.

3. SOFFRITTO: Heat the butter and oil in a heavy 4-quart casserole over moderate heat. Add the onion and sauté for 1 to 2 minutes, until it begins to soften, being careful not to brown it.

4. RISO: Add the rice to the soffritto; using a wooden spoon, stir for 1 minute, making sure all the grains are well coated. Begin to add the simmering broth, ½ cup at a time, stirring frequently. Wait until each addition is almost completely absorbed before adding the next ½ cup, reserving about ¼ cup to add at the end. Stir frequently to prevent sticking.

5. After approximately 18 minutes, when the rice is tender but still firm, turn off the heat. Add the reserved broth. Stir vigorously to combine with the rice. Serve immediately with swordfish ragoût on each serving. Garnish with fresh parsley.

Serves 4

Fish Purée

═══════

RISOTTO
ALLA CHIOGGIOTTA

Chioggia is a small fishing port at the southern tip of the lagoon of Venice, where the local fish, *gò,* is added to risotto as a creamy light purée. You can use any white-fleshed fish, such as cod or halibut; wolffish and cusk are also good choices. This risotto is a wonderful first course, followed by a seafood entrée. Serve with a chilled crisp white wine such as Orvieto.

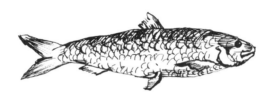

CONDIMENTI	8 ounces firm white-fleshed fish, such as cod, halibut, or wolffish
	¼ cup light cream
	Salt and freshly ground black pepper
	2 tablespoons unsalted butter
	¼ cup grated Parmesan cheese
	1 tablespoon chopped fresh parsley
BRODO	5½ cups Basic Fish Broth (see page 17), approximately
	½ cup dry white wine or broth

SOFFRITTO	2 tablespoons unsalted butter
	1 tablespoon oil
	⅓ cup finely minced onion
	2 tablespoons finely minced carrot
	2 tablespoons finely minced celery
RISO	1½ cups Arborio rice

1. CONDIMENTI: Place the fish in a small saucepan with just enough fish broth to cover. Bring to a boil, turn the heat to moderate-low, and simmer for 10 minutes, until the fish flakes apart easily with a fork. Strain the liquid into the saucepan with the broth. Place the fish in the container of a food processor or blender with the cream and process until smooth. Add salt and pepper to taste. Set aside.

2. BRODO: Bring the broth with the strained poaching liquid to a steady simmer in a saucepan on top of the stove.

3. SOFFRITTO: Heat the butter and oil in a heavy 4-quart casserole over moderate heat. Add the onion, carrot, and celery and sauté for 1 to 2 minutes, until it begins to soften, being careful not to brown it.

4. RISO: Add the rice to the soffritto; using a wooden spoon, stir for 1 minute, making sure all the grains are well coated. Add the wine and stir until it is completely absorbed. Begin to add the simmering broth, ½ cup at a time, stirring frequently. Wait until each addition is almost completely absorbed before adding the next ½ cup, reserving about ¼ cup to add at the end. Stir frequently to prevent sticking.

5. After approximately 18 minutes, when the rice is tender but still firm, add the reserved broth and the condimenti—the fish purée. Turn off the heat and immediately add the butter, Parmesan, and parsley, and stir vigorously to combine with the rice. Serve immediately.

Serves 4

Fresh Tuna & Curry

RISOTTO
CON IL TONNO AL CURRY

The robust flavor of the fresh tuna combines with tomato, curry, and saffron to create an outstanding and colorful risotto that tastes as delicious as it looks. Serve as a second course to follow an antipasto of fresh vegetables dressed with olive oil and lemon juice.

CONDIMENTI	2 tablespoons unsalted butter
	3 tablespoons finely chopped carrot
	3 tablespoons finely chopped celery
	1 small onion, sliced
	1 cup dry white wine
	1 teaspoon salt
	Freshly ground black pepper
	8 ounces fresh tuna steak
	2 tablespoons chopped fresh parsley
BRODO	5 cups poaching liquid, approximately (recipe follows)

SOFFRITTO	2 tablespoons unsalted butter
	1 tablespoon oil
	⅓ cup finely minced onion
	2 small tomatoes, preferably plum tomatoes, peeled, seeded, and coarsely chopped, or ½ cup canned Italian tomatoes, well drained and chopped
	1 teaspoon curry powder
	Pinch of saffron threads, pulverized
RISO	1½ cups Arborio rice

1. CONDIMENTI: Heat the butter in a medium-size saucepan over moderate heat. Add the carrot, celery, and onion and sauté for 3 to 5 minutes, until the vegetables have softened. Add 5 cups of water with the wine, salt, and pepper to taste, and simmer for 15 minutes. Turn the heat to low, place the fish in the saucepan, cover, and poach for 12 minutes, until the fish flakes easily with a fork. Take the fish out of the saucepan, cut it into small uniform pieces, and set aside.

2. BRODO: Strain the liquid in which the fish was poached (there should be approximately 5 cups) and bring it to a steady simmer in a saucepan on top of the stove.

3. SOFFRITTO: Heat the butter and oil in a heavy 4-quart casserole over moderate heat. Add the onion and sauté for 1 to 2 minutes, until it begins to soften, being careful not to brown it. Add the tomatoes, curry powder, and saffron, and continue to cook for 1 to 2 minutes longer.

4. RISO: Add the rice to the soffritto; using a wooden spoon, stir for 1 minute, making sure all the grains are well coated. Begin to add the simmering broth, ½ cup at a time, stirring frequently. Wait until each addition is almost completely absorbed before adding the next ½ cup, reserving about ¼ cup to add at the end. Stir frequently to prevent sticking.

5. After approximately 18 minutes, when the rice is tender but still firm, turn off the heat and immediately add the reserved broth and the condimenti—tuna and parsley—and stir vigorously to combine with the rice. Serve immediately.

Serves 4

VARIATION

Substitute fresh swordfish for the tuna.

Canned Tuna

RISOTTO
AL TONNATO

There are many variations for preparing risotto with canned tuna. The most basic one calls for a simple combination of tuna and Parmesan. We have also tasted a *risotto al tonno sott'olio* (tuna packed in oil), made with tomatoes and basil. We created this recipe with the ingredients and flavorings traditionally used in *tonnato* sauce for cold sliced veal. The pungent flavors of the anchovies and capers combine with the egg yolks to raise the lowly can of tuna to new heights.

BRODO   5½ cups Basic Fish Broth (see page 17), approximately

1 bay leaf

½ cup dry white wine or broth

SOFFRITTO	3 tablespoons olive oil
	⅓ cup finely minced onion
	2 small garlic cloves, finely minced
	3 tablespoons finely minced carrot
	3 tablespoons finely minced celery
	3 flat anchovy fillets, drained
RISO	1½ cups Arborio rice
CONDIMENTI	1 can (6½ ounces) white meat tuna, packed in oil or water, well drained
	3 tablespoons capers, drained
	2 egg yolks, lightly beaten
	2 tablespoons chopped fresh parsley

1. BRODO: Bring the broth with the bay leaf to a steady simmer in a saucepan on top of the stove.

2. SOFFRITTO: Heat the oil in a heavy 4-quart casserole over moderate heat. Add the onion, garlic, carrot, celery, and anchovies and sauté, while mashing the anchovies, for 1 to 2 minutes, until the onion begins to soften, being careful not to brown it.

3. RISO: Add the rice to the soffritto; using a wooden spoon, stir for 1 minute, making sure all the grains are well coated. Add the wine and stir until it is completely absorbed.

4. CONDIMENTI: Add the tuna and begin to add the simmering broth, ½ cup at a time, stirring frequently. Wait until each addition is almost completely absorbed before adding the next ½ cup, reserving about ¼ cup to add at the end. Stir frequently to prevent sticking.

5. After approximately 18 minutes, when the rice is tender but still firm, add the reserved broth. Turn off the heat and add remaining condimenti—capers, egg yolks, and parsley—and stir vigorously to combine with the rice. Serve immediately.

Serves 4

Black Caviar

RISOTTO
AL CAVIALE

The Po River is not only Italy's source of irrigation for the rice fields but is also home to the great sturgeon, which produces that extraordinary delicacy, caviar. The use of caviar in Italian cooking goes back to medieval times. We have prepared this recipe with a variety of native American caviars, since imported brands are prohibitively expensive. We settled on black sturgeon caviar because the tiny eggs are the least salty, and they lend an ever so delicate fishy flavor while retaining their firmness. The cream gives this risotto a perfect smooth texture and the lemon juice adds just the right contrast of flavors.

CONDIMENTI	⅓ cup light cream
	2 ounces black American sturgeon caviar (see Note)
	¼ cup fresh lemon juice

BRODO	5½ cups Basic Fish Broth (see page 17), approximately

SOFFRITTO	2 tablespoons unsalted butter
	1 tablespoon oil
	⅓ cup finely minced onion

RISO	1½ cups Arborio rice

1. CONDIMENTI: Combine the cream with the caviar and set aside.

2. BRODO: Bring the broth to a steady simmer in a saucepan on top of the stove.

3. SOFFRITTO: Heat the butter and oil in a heavy 4-quart casserole over moderate heat. Add the onion and sauté for 1 to 2 minutes, until it begins to soften, being careful not to brown it.

4. RISO: Add the rice to the soffritto; using a wooden spoon, stir for 1 minute, making sure all the grains are well coated. Begin to add the simmering broth, ½ cup at a time, stirring frequently. Wait until each addition is almost completely absorbed before adding the next ½ cup, reserving about ¼ cup to add at the end. Stir frequently to prevent sticking.

5. After approximately 18 minutes, when the rice is tender but still firm, add the reserved broth and the condimenti—caviar and cream mixture and lemon juice—and stir vigorously to combine with the rice. Serve immediately.

Serves 4

NOTE: Fresh caviar is available through fishmarkets and some specialty food stores. It must be refrigerated and should be consumed within a day or two of opening the container. Buy only as much as you will use at once. You can substitute other American caviars, such as golden or red salmon roe; however, we cannot recommend the widely available black lumpfish caviar. It is dyed a black color, which turns the rice an unappetizing gray and is overly salty.

Anchovy

RISOTTO
CON LE ACCIUGHE

One of our favorite ways to eat anchovies is in a traditional Caesar salad with garlic, parsley, and Parmesan. We found that this trio is also perfectly matched for risotto. The much misunderstood salty anchovy has the surprising capacity to become mild and mellow when it's cooked, so additional anchovies go in at the end for more flavor. Serve this as a first course before *involtini alla spada,* a swordfish kabob that's been grilled on a skewer with zucchini and onion.

BRODO	5 cups Basic Fish Broth (see page 17), approximately
	½ cup dry white wine or broth
SOFFRITTO	2 tablespoons unsalted butter
	1 tablespoon oil from anchovy fillets
	⅓ cup finely minced onion

| | 1 garlic clove, finely minced |
| | 6 flat anchovy fillets |

| RISO | 1½ cups Arborio rice |

CONDIMENTI	3 flat anchovy fillets, minced
	1 tablespoon unsalted butter
	¼ cup grated Parmesan cheese
	2 tablespoons chopped fresh parsley

1. BRODO: Bring the broth to a steady simmer in a saucepan on top of the stove.

2. SOFFRITTO: Heat the butter and oil in a heavy 4-quart casserole over moderate heat. Add the onion, garlic, and 6 anchovy fillets. Using a wooden spoon, mash the anchovies. Sauté for 1 to 2 minutes, until the onion begins to soften, being careful not to brown it.

3. RISO: Add the rice to the soffritto; using a wooden spoon, stir for 1 minute, making sure all the grains are well coated. Add the wine and stir until it is completely absorbed. Begin to add the simmering broth, ½ cup at a time, stirring frequently. Wait under each addition is almost completely absorbed before adding the next ½ cup, reserving about ¼ cup to add at the end. Stir frequently to prevent sticking.

4. CONDIMENTI: After approximately 18 minutes, when the rice is tender but still firm, add the reserved broth. Turn off the heat and immediately add the condimenti—minced anchovies, butter, Parmesan, and parsley—and stir vigorously to combine with the rice. Serve immediately.

Serves 4

Eel

RISOTTO
CON L'ANGUILLA ALLA VENETA

Throughout the regions of Northern Italy, risotto is made with the baby eels (elvers) that thrive and grow in the lakes and rivers there. There are risotti that call for a combination of eel with other freshwater fish, such as lake prawns and carp, while some recipes allow the delicious taste of the eel (which most resembles trout) to stand on its own. This is our version of a Venetian risotto made just with eel. We like to prepare it around Christmastime when young small elvers are readily available.

CONDIMENTI	1 eel, 10 to 12 ounces
	1 onion, peeled and left whole
	1 celery rib
	1 bay leaf
	Salt and freshly ground black pepper
BRODO	5½ cups eel broth, approximately (see step 1 below)
SOFFRITTO	3 tablespoons oil
	⅓ cup finely minced onion
	1 garlic clove, finely minced
	¼ cup chopped fresh parsley
RISO	1½ cups Arborio rice

1. CONDIMENTI: Place the eel with 2 quarts of water in a large 4-quart saucepan over high heat. Add the onion, celery, bay leaf, and salt and pepper to taste, and bring to a boil. Turn the heat to moderate-low and simmer for 20 minutes. Remove eel and strain and reserve liquid (eel broth). Place the eel on a cutting board. Cut off and discard the head; make a slit down one side of the eel, and carefully remove the skin and bones. Cut the meat into small pieces and set aside.

2. BRODO: Bring the eel broth to a steady simmer in a saucepan on top of the stove.

3. SOFFRITTO: Heat the oil in a heavy 4-quart casserole over moderate heat. Add the onion, garlic, and parsley, and sauté for 1 to 2 minutes, until the onion begins to soften, being careful not to brown it.

4. RISO: Add the rice to the soffritto; using a wooden spoon, stir for 1 minute, making sure all the grains are well coated. Begin to add the simmering broth, ½ cup at a time, stirring frequently. Wait until each addition is almost completely absorbed before adding the next ½ cup, reserving about ¼ cup to add at the end. Stir frequently to prevent sticking.

5. When the rice has been cooking 10 minutes, add the eel and continue to add the broth. After approximately 18 minutes, when the rice is tender but still firm, add the reserved broth and and stir vigorously to combine with the rice. Serve immediately.

Serves 4

Frog's Legs

RISOTTO
CON RANE

Risotto with frog's legs is a specialty of Pavia in Lombardy. This version, with pancetta and fresh peas, was created by Todd English, the chef at Michela's, a Northern Italian restaurant in Cambridge, Massachusetts. Frog's legs are available through specialty fish and even some meat markets. If you can only get small legs, increase the quantity to three or even four pairs.

SOFFRITTO	4 tablespoons unsalted butter
	⅓ cup finely chopped onion
	¼ cup finely chopped pancetta
	1 tablespoon fresh thyme
	½ teaspoon chopped garlic
CONDIMENTI	2 pairs fresh frog's legs, deboned, the meat diced
	2 tablespoons unsalted butter
	1 cup fresh shelled peas or defrosted frozen peas, not cooked
	⅓ cup grated Parmesan cheese
RISO	1½ cups Arborio rice
BRODO	½ cup dry white wine
	5 cups Chicken Broth (see page 15), approximately

1. SOFFRITTO: Heat the butter in a heavy 4-quart casserole over moderate heat. Add the onion, pancetta, thyme, and garlic, and sauté for about 1 to 2 minutes, until the onion begins to soften, being careful not to brown it.

2. CONDIMENTI: Add the frog's legs and stir to combine with the soffritto.

3. RISO: Add the rice to the frog's legs and soffritto; using a wooden spoon, stir for 1 minute, making sure all the grains are well coated.

4. BRODO: Add the wine and stir until it is completely absorbed. Begin to add the simmering broth, ½ cup at a time, stirring frequently. Wait until each addition is almost completely absorbed before adding the next ½ cup, reserving about ¼ cup to add at the end. Stir frequently to prevent sticking.

5. After approximately 18 minutes, when the rice is tender but still firm, add the reserved broth. Turn off the heat and immediately add the remaining condimenti—butter, peas, and Parmesan cheese—and stir vigorously to combine with the rice. Serve immediately.

Serves 4

Seafood Risotti

Shrimp & Peas

RISOTTO
CON GAMBERETTI E PISELLI

In Italian seaside cities, it's not uncommon to encounter a Risotto con Gamberetti that is heavily flavored but only sparsely endowed with seafood. Our version, adapted for a main course, is abundant with shrimp. Serve after a first course of steamed fresh vegetables dressed only with oil, salt, and pepper.

BRODO	5 cups Shrimp Broth (recipe follows) or Basic Fish Broth (see page 17), approximately
	½ cup dry white wine or broth
SOFFRITTO	2 tablespoons unsalted butter
	1 tablespoon oil
	⅓ cup finely minced onion
	1 garlic clove, finely minced
RISO	1½ cups Arborio rice
CONDIMENTI	12 ounces small shrimp, shelled and deveined (reserve shells for broth)
	1 tablespoon unsalted butter
	½ cup fresh peas or defrosted frozen peas, not cooked

1. **BRODO:** Prepare the broth and bring to a steady simmer in a saucepan on top of the stove.

2. **SOFFRITTO:** Heat the butter and oil in a heavy 4-quart casserole over moderate heat. Add the onion and garlic and sauté for 1 to 2 minutes, until the onion begins to soften, being careful not to brown it.

3. **RISO:** Add the rice to the soffritto; using a wooden spoon, stir for 1 minute, making sure all the grains are well coated. Add the wine and stir until it is completely absorbed. Begin to add the simmering broth, ½ cup at a time, stirring frequently. Wait until each addition is almost completely absorbed before adding the next ½ cup, reserving about ¼ cup to add at the end. Stir frequently to prevent sticking.

4. **CONDIMENTI:** Add the shrimp after the rice has been cooking for about 10 minutes, and continue to add the broth, ½ cup at a time.

5. After approximately 18 minutes, when the rice is tender but still firm, add the reserved broth and the remaining condimenti—butter and peas—and stir vigorously to combine with the rice. Serve immediately.

Serves 4

Shrimp Broth/brodo di gamberetti

2 cups shells from shrimp, approximately

1 small yellow onion, peeled and left whole

2 celery ribs

3 fresh parsley sprigs

6 cups water

1 tablespoon salt

Combine all the ingredients in a large saucepan. Bring the water to a boil and simmer for 20 minutes. Strain liquid.

VARIATION

In Stresa, the resort town on Lake Maggiore, we tasted a risotto of shrimp that was laced with yellow squash blossoms. If you are lucky enough to grow your own zucchini, or have a source for the blossoms, since they are not readily sold in most markets, add 3 to 4 ounces chopped cleaned blossoms (stems and pistils removed) to the risotto when you add the shrimp. They have only a mild vegetable flavor, but they transform this risotto into a very special delicacy.

Shrimp & Squash

RISOTTO
CON GAMBERETTI E ZUCCA

We discovered this risotto in Milan at a wonderful restaurant called La Scaletta, which is owned by Aldo Bellini and his mother, Pina. They have created a very personal style of Italian cooking, which relies on daring combinations of ingredients for spectacular effects. With this risotto, the Bellinis made the unusual pairing of sweet squash with shrimp, topped with shavings of white truffle. The results were delicate and delicious. In our version we have made the white truffle an optional choice; if it is available, use it, but the risotto will be excellent either way.

CONDIMENTI	4 ounces butternut squash, peeled, seeded, and cut into small pieces
	8 ounces small shrimp, shelled and deveined
	¼ cup light cream
	2 tablespoons grated Parmesan cheese
	1 tablespoon chopped fresh parsley
	1 white truffle, shaved (optional) (see page 157 for instructions on shaving truffles)
BRODO	5 cups Basic Fish Broth (see page 17), approximately
	½ cup dry white wine
SOFFRITTO	2 tablespoons unsalted butter
	1 tablespoon oil
	⅓ cup finely minced onion
RISO	1½ cups Arborio rice

1. CONDIMENTI: Place the squash in a small saucepan with water to cover. Bring to a boil and cook for about 10 minutes, until squash is tender when pierced with a knife. Drain and place in the container of a food processor or blender with ¼ cup of the water in which it was cooked, and process until smooth. Set aside.

2. BRODO: Bring the broth to a steady simmer in a saucepan on top of the stove.

3. SOFFRITTO: Heat the butter and oil in a heavy 4-quart casserole over moderate heat. Add the onion and sauté for 1 to 2 minutes, until it begins to soften, being careful not to brown it.

4. RISO: Add the rice to the soffritto; using a wooden spoon, stir for 1 minute, making sure all the grains are well coated. Add the wine and stir until it is completely absorbed. Begin to add the simmering broth, ½ cup at a time, stirring frequently. Wait until each addition is almost completely absorbed before adding the next ½ cup, reserving about ¼ cup to add at the end. Stir frequently to prevent sticking.

5. Add the shrimp and squash after the rice has been cooking for 10 minutes, and continue to add the broth, ½ cup at a time. After approximately 18 minutes, when the rice is tender but still firm, add the reserved broth and the remaining condimenti—cream, Parmesan, and parsley—and stir vigorously to combine with the rice. Serve immediately. If you are using the white truffle, place some of the truffle shavings on each serving.

Serves 4

Scallops, Shrimp, & Mushrooms

RISOTTO
MARI E MONTI

This risotto captures the best of the sea *(mari)* and the mountains *(monti)*; the fresh seafood, wild mushrooms, and cream create a particularly rich first course. Follow with flavorful veal scaloppine in a lemon or wine sauce.

CONDIMENTI	2 tablespoons unsalted butter
	1 garlic clove, finely minced
	4 ounces white mushrooms (shiitake, oyster, or similar), stems removed, sliced, to make about 2 cups
	4 ounces scallops
	4 ounces medium shrimp, shelled and deveined
	½ cup light cream
	1 tablespoon chopped fresh parsley
BRODO	5 cups Basic Fish Broth (see page 17), approximately
	½ cup dry white wine or broth
SOFFRITTO	2 tablespoons unsalted butter
	1 tablespoon oil
	⅓ cup finely minced onion
RISO	1½ cups Arborio rice

1. CONDIMENTI: Heat the butter in a skillet over moderate heat. When it begins to foam, add the garlic and mushrooms and sauté for 1 to 2 minutes, until the mushrooms begin to soften. Add the scallops and shrimp and continue cooking for 2 to 3 minutes longer. Add the cream and simmer for about 5 minutes, until it has thickened slightly. Stir in the parsley and set aside.

2. BRODO: Bring the broth to a steady simmer in a saucepan on top of the stove.

3. SOFFRITTO: Heat the butter and oil in a heavy 4-quart casserole over moderate heat. Add the onion and sauté for 1 to 2 minutes,

until it begins to soften, being careful not to brown it.

4. RISO: Add the rice to the soffritto; using a wooden spoon, stir for 1 minute, making sure all the grains are well coated. Add the wine and stir until it is completely absorbed. Begin to add the simmering broth, ½ cup at a time, stirring frequently. Wait until each addition is almost completely absorbed before adding the next ½ cup. Stir frequently to prevent sticking.

5. After approximately 18 minutes, when the rice is tender but still firm, add the condimenti—the seafood-mushroom-cream mixture—and stir vigorously to combine with the rice. Serve immediately.

Serves 4

Scallops & Saffron

RISOTTO
GIALLO ALLE CAPESANTE

The combination of scallops, cream, and saffron creates a colorful risotto with a delicious, rich taste. This risotto is at the top of our list of favorite ways to prepare scallops. Serve with steamed asparagus or a simple green salad of Bibb lettuce and endive.

CONDIMENTI	2 tablespoons finely minced shallots
	2 small tomatoes, peeled, seeded, and chopped, or ½ cup canned Italian tomatoes, well drained and chopped
	½ teaspoon powdered saffron
	½ cup dry white wine
	8 ounces small bay scallops (if only sea scallops are available, cut them into quarters)
	½ cup light cream
	Salt and freshly ground black pepper
	2 tablespoons chopped fresh parsley
BRODO	5 cups Basic Fish Broth (see page 17), approximately
	½ cup dry white wine or broth
SOFFRITTO	2 tablespoons unsalted butter
	1 tablespoon oil
	¼ cup finely minced onion
RISO	1½ cups Arborio rice

1. CONDIMENTI: Combine the shallots, tomatoes, saffron, and wine in a saucepan over moderate heat. Bring the wine to a boil, add the scallops, and cook for 2 minutes, or until scallops turn opaque. Remove scallops from the cooking liquid and set aside. Turn the heat to high and bring the liquid back to a boil; simmer until it is reduced to about half. Add the cream to the reduced scallop liquid and continue cooking for 2 to 3 minutes, until the liquid has thickened slightly. Turn off the heat. Return the scallops to the saucepan, taste for salt and pepper, and set aside.

2. BRODO: Bring the broth to a steady simmer in a saucepan on top of the stove.

3. SOFFRITTO: Heat the butter and oil in a heavy 4-quart casserole over moderate heat. Add the onion and sauté for 1 to 2 minutes, until it begins to soften, being careful not to brown it.

4. RISO: Add the rice to the soffritto; using a wooden spoon, stir for 1 minute, making sure all the grains are well coated. Add the wine and stir until it is completely absorbed. Begin to add to simmering broth, ½ cup at a time, stirring frequently. Wait until each addition is almost completely absorbed before adding the next ½ cup. Stir frequently to prevent sticking.

5. After approximately 18 minutes, when the rice is tender but still firm, add the condimenti—the scallop-tomato-cream mixture and the parsley—and stir vigorously to combine with the rice. Serve immediately.

Serves 4

Lobster

RISOTTO ALL'ARAGOSTA

Lobster can transform any meal into a celebration. This risotto is one way to get some extra mileage out of two small lobsters. For the most flavor you should ideally prepare a broth from the lobster shells (see Note). For a short cut, buy cooked lobster meat or frozen lobster and use the Basic Fish Broth. This risotto, served with a sparkling dry white wine, can surely be a festive and elegant main course.

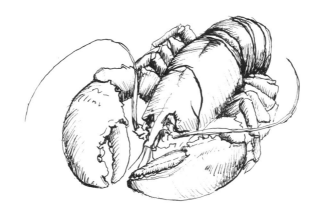

CONDIMENTI	1 tablespoon unsalted butter
	1 garlic clove, finely minced
	1 small tomato, peeled, seeded, and chopped, or ¼ cup canned Italian tomatoes, well drained and chopped
	8 ounces cooked lobster meat from two 1½-pound lobsters or 3 "chicken" (1-pound) lobsters (for preparation, see Note below), or defrosted lobster tails
	2 tablespoons unsalted butter
	1 tablespoon chopped fresh parsley

BRODO	5 cups Lobster Broth (see Note for recipe), approximately, or Basic Fish Broth (see page 17)
	½ cup dry white wine

SOFFRITTO	2 tablespoons unsalted butter
	1 tablespoon oil
	2 tablespoons finely minced onion

1 tablespoon finely minced carrot

1 tablespoon finely minced celery

RISO   1½ cups Arborio rice

1. CONDIMENTI: Heat the butter in a small skillet over moderate heat. When it begins to foam, add the garlic and tomato and cook for about 1 minute, until the tomato begins to soften and lose its red color. Add the lobster, stir to combine it with the tomato, and gently sauté for 3 to 5 minutes, until the lobster is heated through. Turn off the heat and set aside.

2. BRODO: Prepare the lobster broth as directed (or Basic Fish Broth) and bring to a steady simmer in a saucepan on top of the stove.

3. SOFFRITTO: Heat the butter and oil in a heavy 4-quart casserole over moderate heat. Add the onion, carrot, and celery and sauté for 1 to 2 minutes, until the onion begins to soften, being careful not to brown it.

4. RISO: Add the rice to the soffritto; using a wooden spoon, stir for 1 minute, making sure all the grains are well coated. Add the wine and stir until it is completely absorbed. Begin to add the simmering broth, ½ cup at a time, stirring frequently. Wait until each addition is almost completely absorbed before adding the next ½ cup, reserving about ¼ cup to add at the end. Stir frequently to prevent sticking.

5. After approximately 18 minutes, when the rice is tender but still firm, add the reserved broth and the condimenti—the lobster, butter, and parsley—and stir vigorously to combine with the rice. Serve immediately.

Serves 4

NOTE: *To prepare lobster meat and broth:* In a pot large enough to hold the lobsters, bring 4 cups of water to a boil over high heat. Quickly place the live lobsters in the pot, cover, and cook for 10 minutes for 1-pound lobsters, 15 minutes for 1½-pounders. Turn off the heat. Take the lobsters from the pot and allow them to become cool enough to handle.

Remove the lobster meat from the tail and claws and reserve. Return the shells to the pot with an additional 6 cups of water, 1 onion, 1 carrot, 2 celery ribs, a few parsley sprigs, and 1 tablespoon salt. Bring to a boil and simmer for 20 minutes. Strain the liquid. It is now ready to be added to the risotto.

VARIATION

Substitute medium-size shrimp, shelled and deveined, for half or all of the lobster.

Squid

RISOTTO
NERO ALLE SEPPIE

Black risotto made with squid and its ink is a traditional Venetian specialty. "This dish," according to Giuseppe Mazzotti, one of Italy's most celebrated contemporary writers on gastronomy, "causes the brows of novices to knit suspiciously, and their noses to wrinkle; nevertheless, at the second mouthful, they almost always allow themselves to be conquered by the rare flavor of this dish, alarming as it is to the eye." And it's true; everyone we've served it to approaches the glossy black rice with great caution, but in short order the wonderful flavor overpowers any hesitations. We find this risotto makes a dramatic and ample main course. Follow with a simple salad of fresh arugula, red-leaf lettuce, and scallions.

BRODO	Ink from 4 squid (see Note)
	5½ cups water
	1 medium-size onion
	1 celery rib
	1 tablespoon salt
SOFFRITTO	3 tablespoons olive oil
	⅓ cup finely minced onion
	1 large or 2 small garlic cloves, finely minced
	1 tablespoon chopped fresh parsley
RISO	1½ cups Arborio rice
CONDIMENTI	8 ounces cleaned squid, cut into small pieces (see Note)

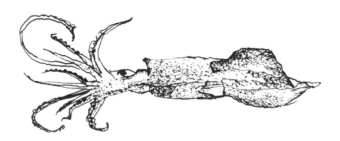

1. BRODO: Remove the ink sacs from the squid and squeeze out the ink into a small saucepan. Discard the sacs. Combine the ink with the water, onion, celery, and salt, and bring to a steady simmer on top of the stove.

2. SOFFRITTO: Heat the oil in a heavy 4-quart casserole over moderate heat. Add the onion, garlic, and parsley and sauté for 1 to 2 minutes, until the onion begins to soften, being careful not to brown it.

3. RISO: Add the rice to the soffritto; using a wooden spoon, stir for 1 minute, making sure all the grains are well coated. Begin to add the simmering broth, ½ cup at a time, stirring frequently. Wait until each addition is almost completely absorbed before adding the next ½ cup, reserving about ¼ cup to add at the end. Stir frequently to prevent sticking.

4. CONDIMENTI: After approximately 15 minutes, when the rice is tender but still firm, add the squid and cook for 3 minutes longer. Add the reserved broth and stir vigorously to combine with the rice. Serve immediately.

Serves 4

NOTE: To clean a squid, pull the head and body of the squid apart and cut off the tentacles just below the eyes. Reserve the tentacles and the dark sac that contains the ink. Remove and discard the transparent quill from the inside of the body. Rinse the body well to remove the milky substance inside, and peel and discard the purple-grayish membrane covering it.

Squid & Artichokes

RISOTTO
AI CALAMARI E CARCIOFI

The squid without its ink lends a more subtle flavor and rosy color to the rice, which highlights the artichokes in this extraordinary risotto. Serve this as a second course preceded by thin-sliced raw tuna *carpaccio*.

CONDIMENTI	2 whole squid, cleaned (see Risotto Nero alle Seppie for instructions on cleaning squid)
	1 medium-size artichoke, trimmed, choke removed, and sliced into small pieces (see Artichoke Risotto for directions)
	3 tablespoons olive oil
	1 tablespoon finely minced onion
	1 garlic clove, finely minced
	½ cup Basic Fish Broth (see page 17)
	Salt and freshly ground black pepper
	Pinch of peperoncino (hot red pepper flakes)
	1 tablespoon chopped fresh parsley
BRODO	5½ cups Basic Fish Broth (see page 17), approximately
SOFFRITTO	2 tablespoons unsalted butter
	1 tablespoon oil
	2 tablespoons finely minced onion
RISO	1½ cups Arborio rice

1. CONDIMENTI: Cut the cleaned squid into ½-inch pieces. Prepare artichoke and slice as directed. Heat the oil in a skillet over moderate heat, add the onion and garlic, and cook for 1 to 2 minutes, until the onion begins to soften. Add the artichoke and ½ cup fish broth. Cover and simmer for 10 to 15 minutes, until artichoke is tender and the fish broth has evaporated. Add the squid and cook for 3 to 5 minutes, until squid turns opaque. Add salt and pepper to taste. Turn off the heat and set aside.

2. *BRODO:* Bring the broth to a steady simmer in a saucepan on top of the stove.

3. *SOFFRITTO:* Heat the butter and oil in a heavy 4-quart casserole over moderate heat. Add the onion and sauté for 1 to 2 minutes, until it begins to soften, being careful not to brown it.

4. *RISO:* Add the rice to the soffritto; using a wooden spoon, stir for 1 minute, making sure all the grains are well coated. Add the wine and stir until it is completely absorbed. Begin to add the simmering broth, ½ cup at at time, stirring frequently. Wait until each addition is almost completely absorbed before adding the next ½ cup, reserving about ¼ cup to add at the end. Stir frequently to prevent sticking.

5. After approximately 18 minutes, when the rice is tender but still firm, add the reserved broth and the condimenti—squid and artichoke, peperoncino, and parsley—and stir vigorously to combine with the rice. Serve immediately.

Serves 4

Mussels in White Wine

RISOTTO
CON COZZE E VINO BIANCO

Every bit of mussel flavor is captured in this risotto, since the broth used is made only from the steamed mussels and wine. After steaming the mussels, be sure to strain the broth thoroughly through a clean dishtowel or several thicknesses of cheesecloth to remove any sand that collects in the bottom of the pot. Serve this risotto after an antipasto of thin-sliced zucchini and sweet red pepper sautéed in oil and garlic.

BRODO	2 pounds mussels, scrubbed
	1 bottle (750 ml) dry white wine, or 3 cups bottled clam juice
	¼ cup finely minced shallots
	1 garlic clove, finely minced
	1 tablespoon chopped fresh parsley
SOFFRITTO	2 tablespoons unsalted butter
	1 tablespoon oil
	⅓ cup finely minced onion
	1 garlic clove, finely minced
RISO	1½ cups Arborio rice
CONDIMENTI	1 tablespoon unsalted butter
	⅓ cup grated Parmesan cheese
	¼ cup chopped fresh parsley

1. *BRODO:* Place the scrubbed mussels with the wine, shallots, garlic, and parsley in a large saucepan; the pot must have enough room to accommodate the shells after they open. Set the pan over moderate-high heat, cover, bring to a boil, then lower the heat to moderate and cook for 5 to 10 minutes, until the mussel shells have opened. Remove the mussel meat from shells, reserving enough mussels in their shells to have one for a garnish on each serving, and set aside. Discard any mussels that have not opened. Strain liquid through several thicknesses of cheesecloth or a dishtowel into a saucepan and bring it to a steady simmer on top of the stove.

2. *SOFFRITTO:* Heat the butter and oil in a heavy 4-quart casserole over moderate heat. Add the onion and garlic and sauté for 1 to 2 minutes, until the onion begins to soften, being careful not to brown it.

3. *RISO:* Add the rice to the soffritto; using a wooden spoon, stir for 1 minute, making sure all the grains are well coated. Begin to add the simmering broth, ½ cup at a time, stirring frequently. Wait until each addition is almost completely absorbed before adding the next ½ cup, reserving about ¼ cup to add at the end. Stir frequently to prevent sticking.

4. *CONDIMENTI:* After approximately 18 minutes, when the rice is tender but still firm, add the reserved broth and the mussels. Turn off the heat and immediately add the condimenti—butter, Parmesan, and parsley—and stir vigorously to combine with the rice. Serve immediately.

Serves 4

Clams, Tomatoes, & Red Wine

RISOTTO
ROSSO ALLE VONGOLE

This risotto calls for minced clams because their fine texture most closely resembles the tiny *vongole* you find in Italy. If you want to use whole, not minced, clams, we recommend the smallest Little Necks, which should be steamed and removed from their shells before proceeding with the directions. The red wine gives the clams and tomatoes a rich full-bodied flavor. Serve this risotto as a first course before an entrée of grilled fish or as a light summer meal in itself with a salad of greens and some crusty sourdough bread.

CONDIMENTI	1 tablespoon olive oil
	1 tablespoon minced onion
	1 garlic clove, finely minced
	2 small plum tomatoes, peeled, seeded, and chopped, or ½ cup canned Italian tomatoes, well drained and chopped
	8 ounces minced clams, about 1 cup, with their juices (see Note)
	½ cup light-tasting red wine, such as Bardolino
	Salt and freshly ground black pepper
	2 tablespoons grated Parmesan cheese
	1 tablespoon chopped fresh parsley
BRODO	5½ cups Basic Fish Broth (see page 17), approximately

SOFFRITTO	2 tablespoons unsalted butter
	1 tablespoon oil
	2 tablespoons finely minced onion
RISO	1½ cups Arborio rice

1. CONDIMENTI: Heat the oil with the minced onion and garlic in a skillet over moderate heat and cook for 1 to 2 minutes, until the onion begins to soften. Add the tomatoes and continue cooking for 2 to 3 minutes, until the tomatoes begin to soften and lose their red color. Add the wine, turn the heat to high, and cook vigorously until the liquid in the pan has been reduced to a few tablespoons. Stir in the clams. Add salt and pepper to taste. Turn off the heat and set aside.

2. BRODO: Bring the broth to a steady simmer in a saucepan on top of the stove.

3. SOFFRITTO: Heat the butter and oil in a heavy 4-quart casserole over moderate heat. Add the onion and sauté for 1 to 2 minutes, until it begins to soften, being careful not to brown it.

4. RISO: Add the rice to the soffritto; using a wooden spoon, stir for 1 minute, making sure all the grains are well coated. Begin to add the simmering broth, ½ cup at a time, stirring frequently. Wait until each addition is almost completely absorbed before adding the next ½ cup, reserving about ¼ cup to add at the end. Stir frequently to prevent sticking.

5. After approximately 18 minutes, when the rice is tender but still firm, add the reserved broth and the condimenti—the tomatoes and clams, Parmesan, and parsley—and stir vigorously to combine with the rice. Serve immediately.

Serves 4

NOTE: Minced clams are widely available in supermarkets and fishmarkets, fresh, frozen, or canned. To make your own minced clams, buy 1 to 2 pounds (approximately) fresh hard-shelled clams, preferably chowder clams, in their shells. Scrub them and put them in a large saucepan with 1 cup water over moderate-high heat. Bring to a boil, cover, and cook for 5 minutes, or until the shells begin to open. Remove the clams and let stand until they are cool enough to handle. Cut the clams from the shells and chop coarsely.

Clams & Radicchio

RISOTTO
CON VONGOLE E RADICCHIO

Here the tangy twosome of clams and radicchio works in tandem with cream and saffron to create a flavorful as well as colorful dish. As a first course this risotto could precede a delicately sautéed veal or lightly grilled chicken dish.

CONDIMENTI	1 tablespoon unsalted butter
	1 garlic clove, finely minced
	1 tablespoon minced onion
	½ small head of radicchio, shredded (about 1½ cups)
	Pinch of powdered saffron
	½ cup light cream
	8 ounces minced clams, with their juices (see Note on recipe for Clams, Tomatoes, and Red Wine)
	Salt and freshly ground black pepper

| BRODO | 5 cups Basic Fish Broth (see page 17), approximately |
| | ½ cup dry white wine or broth |

SOFFRITTO	2 tablespoons unsalted butter
	1 tablespoon oil
	½ cup finely minced onion

| RISO | 1½ cups Arborio rice |

1. CONDIMENTI: Heat the butter in a skillet over moderate heat. When it begins to foam, add the garlic and onion and sauté for 1 to 2 minutes, until onion begins to soften. Stir in the radicchio and saffron and cook for 3 to 5 minutes longer. Add the cream, turn the heat to moderate-high, and continue cooking until the cream has been reduced by half. Stir in the clams. Add salt and pepper to taste. Turn off the heat and set aside.

2. BRODO: Bring the broth to a steady simmer in a saucepan on top of the stove.

3. SOFFRITTO: Heat the butter and oil in a heavy 4-quart casserole over moderate heat. Add the onion and sauté for 1 to 2 minutes, until it begins to soften, being careful not to brown it.

4. RISO: Add the rice to the soffritto; using a wooden spoon, stir for 1 minute, making sure all the grains are well coated. Begin to add the simmering broth, ½ cup at a time, stirring frequently. Wait until each addition is almost completely absorbed before adding the next ½ cup, reserving about ¼ cup to add at the end. Stir frequently to prevent sticking.

5. After approximately 18 minutes, when the rice is tender but still firm, add the reserved broth and the condimenti—the clams-radicchio-cream mixture—and stir vigorously to combine with the rice. Serve immediately.

Serves 4

Oysters

RISOTTO
CON LE OSTRICHE

The oysters are sautéed with butter and green onion, then simmered in wine to bring out their delicate flavor. If possible, buy shucked oysters at your fishmarket; it makes this easy risotto that much quicker to prepare. Serve this as a first course before grilled fish steaks, with a salad of blanched zucchini and summer squash.

CONDIMENTI	1 tablespoon unsalted butter
	8 oysters, removed from shells and chopped
	2 tablespoons minced green onion (scallion), white part only
	½ cup dry white wine
	Salt and freshly ground black pepper
	¼ cup light cream
	1 tablespoon chopped fresh parsley
BRODO	5½ cups Basic Fish Broth (see page 17), approximately
SOFFRITTO	2 tablespoons unsalted butter
	1 tablespoon oil
	2 tablespoons finely minced onion
RISO	1½ cups Arborio rice

1. CONDIMENTI: Heat the butter in a small skillet over moderate heat. When it begins to foam, add the oysters and green onion and cook gently for 1 to 2 minutes, until the oysters begin to give up their juices. Add the wine, turn the heat to high, and boil vigorously until the liquid in the pan has been reduced to about 1 tablespoon. Add salt and pepper to taste. Turn off the heat and set aside.

2. BRODO: Bring the broth to a steady simmer in a saucepan on top of the stove.

3. SOFFRITTO: Heat the butter and oil in a heavy 4-quart casserole over moderate heat. Add the onion and sauté for 1 to 2 minutes, until it begins to soften, being careful not to brown it.

4. RISO: Add the rice to the soffritto; using a wooden spoon, stir for 1 minute, making sure all the grains are well coated. Begin to add the simmering broth, ½ cup at a time, stirring frequently. Wait until each addition is almost completely absorbed before adding the next ½ cup. Stir frequently to prevent sticking.

5. After approximately 18 minutes, when the rice is tender but still firm, add the condimenti—oysters, cream, and parsley—and stir vigorously to combine with the rice. Serve immediately.

Serves 4

Meat Risotti

MEAT in Italy refers to veal, beef, lamb, poultry, and game as well as *salume*, the Italian name for that group of partially or wholly cured or cooked hams, sausages, and salamis. This chapter includes risotti made with all varieties of meat.

The region around Florence in Tuscany has long been regarded as the premier producer of beef cattle in Italy, and this explains why some meat risotti carry the names "Fiorentina" and "Toscano." Meat risotti are now found in restaurants throughout Italy, such as the Milanese restaurant Giannino, for example, which serves, as one of its house specialties, Risotto al Giannino, a risotto flecked with tiny slivers of beef.

It has been said that there are more poultry dishes in Italian cuisine than any other type of meat. Risotto is also one of the best and most delicious ways to show off the versatility of poultry. In much the same way that risotto itself takes on a different character depending on what *condimenti* are added to it, poultry also adapts well to many different combinations of ingredients and seasonings.

In addition, this section includes the risotti made with *salume,* the general name for those delectable meats such as prosciutto and salami, which have been preserved by air-curing, salt-curing, or smoking. The myriad of uncured flavorful and spicy sausages that come in casings also fall under this heading.

The *risotti di carne* are among the heartiest risotto dishes we offer. Many of the beef, veal, and lamb risotti are actually meat ragùs or stews, which are prepared separately and served alongside the rice rather than combined with it. The risotto is served as an accompaniment; *ossobuco,* braised veal shanks served with Risotto alla Milanese, is the most notable example. When it comes to poultry, to ensure the meat is as tender as can be, chicken and turkey are generally cooked and seasoned separately and added to the finished risotto while sausage and ham are usually cooked along with the rice.

While all the *risotti di carne* are splendid when served as a first course, we find they are natural main courses for luncheon or dinner.

Veal, Mushrooms, & Asparagus

RISOTTO
ALLA MONDINA

Mondina is the old Italian term for a woman rice weeder of the Po Valley. This recipe, filled with lean veal, sliced wild, earthy-tasting mushrooms, and fresh asparagus tips, is a variation of the risotto they prepared during harvesttime. Serve it with crusty bread and a salad of grated carrots on a bed of crisp greens.

CONDIMENTI	2 tablespoons unsalted butter
	6 ounces lean veal scallops, cut into thin strips
	4 ounces shiitake mushrooms, stems removed, sliced (about 2 cups), or 8 ounces cultivated mushrooms
	10 asparagus tips, about 1½ inches long
	Salt and freshly ground black pepper
	2 ounces Italian Fontina cheese, rind removed, cut into small pieces (about 3 tablespoons)
	¼ cup light cream
	Pinch of ground cinnamon
	⅓ cup grated Parmesan cheese

BRODO	5 cups Basic Broth (see page 14), approximately
	½ cup dry white wine or broth

SOFFRITTO	2 tablespoons unsalted butter
	1 tablespoon oil
	⅓ cup finely minced onion

RISO	1½ cups Arborio rice

1. CONDIMENTI: Heat the butter in a skillet over moderate heat. When it begins to foam, add the veal strips, mushrooms, and asparagus, and sauté for 5 to 8 minutes, stirring frequently until veal begins to brown. Add salt and pepper to taste. Set aside.

2. BRODO: Bring the broth to a steady simmer in a saucepan on top of the stove.

3. SOFFRITTO: Heat the butter and oil in a heavy 4-quart casserole over moderate heat. Add the onion and sauté for 1 to 2 minutes, until it begins to soften, being careful not to brown it.

4. RISO: Add the rice to the soffritto; using a wooden spoon, stir for 1 minute, making sure all the grains are well coated. Add the wine and stir until it is completely absorbed. Begin to add the simmering broth, ½ cup at a time, stirring frequently. Wait until each addition is almost completely absorbed before adding the next ½ cup, reserving about ¼ cup to add at the end. Stir frequently to prevent sticking.

5. After approximately 18 minutes, when the rice is tender but still firm, add the reserved broth and the condimenti—the veal-mushroom-asparagus mixture, Fontina, cream, cinnamon, and Parmesan—and stir vigorously to combine with the rice. Serve immediately.

Serves 4

VARIATION

In place of the Fontina, add 3 tablespoons grated Emmentaler cheese and omit the Parmesan and cream.

Veal in White Cream Sauce

RISOTTO
AL RAGÙ BIANCO DI VITELLO

Veal and prosciutto combine with cream to make this a rich and flavorful risotto. Serve as a second course preceded by a colorful salad of blanched baby carrots and broccoli in a lemony dressing.

CONDIMENTI | 2 tablespoons unsalted butter

8 ounces lean veal, ground

2 ounces prosciutto, finely chopped (½ cup)

½ cup light cream

Salt and freshly ground black pepper

⅓ cup grated Parmesan cheese

1 tablespoon finely chopped fresh parsley

BRODO	5 cups Basic Broth (see page 14), approximately
	½ cup dry white wine or broth
SOFFRITTO	2 tablespoons unsalted butter
	1 tablespoon oil
	⅓ cup finely minced onion
RISO	1½ cups Arborio rice

1. CONDIMENTI: Heat the butter in a skillet over moderate heat. When it begins to foam, add the veal and prosciutto; using a fork, break up the meat while sautéing for about 5 minutes, until all the veal loses its pink color. Add the cream and continue cooking for 5 minutes more, until the cream thickens slightly. Add salt and pepper to taste. Turn off heat and set aside.

2. BRODO: Bring the broth to a steady simmer in a saucepan on top of the stove.

3. SOFFRITTO: Heat the butter and oil in a heavy 4-quart casserole over moderate heat. Add the onion and sauté for 1 to 2 minutes, until it begins to soften, being careful not to brown it.

4. RISO: Add the rice to the soffritto; using a wooden spoon, stir for 1 minute, making sure all the grains are well coated. Add the wine and stir until it is completely absorbed. Begin to add the simmering broth, ½ cup at a time, stirring frequently. Wait until each addition is almost completely absorbed before adding the next ½ cup. Stir frequently to prevent sticking.

5. After approximately 18 minutes, when the rice is tender but still firm, add the condimenti—the veal-prosciutto-cream sauce, Parmesan, and parsley—and stir vigorously to combine with the rice. Serve immediately.

Serves 4

Braised Veal Shanks

RISOTTO
CON OSSOBUCO ALLA MILANESE

Ossobuco is a dish of veal shanks cooked until they are so tender that the meat almost melts in the mouth. The custom in Milan is to serve this dish garnished with a *gremolada,* a mixture of minced garlic, lemon rind, and parsley, and accompanied by a serving of glistening yellow Risotto alla Milanese (see Index), flavored with the marrow from the braised shanks. There are many recipes for preparing this wonderful dish, but our favorite is this one, in which the pieces of veal shank are cooked with tomatoes in a rich and flavorful meat broth.

Braised Veal Shanks

VEAL

4 tablespoons unsalted butter

2 ounces pancetta, diced

1 medium-size onion, finely chopped

1 carrot, peeled and finely chopped

1 celery rib, finely chopped

2 whole veal shanks, cut into 2-inch-thick pieces and tied with string (you should end up with 6 to 8 pieces) (See Notes for preparation)

1 cup all-purpose flour

2 tablespoons vegetable oil

1 cup dry white wine

BROTH	2 cups canned Italian tomatoes, coarsely chopped, with their juice
	½ teaspoon dried thyme
	1 bay leaf
	3 fresh parsley sprigs
	2 cups Basic Broth (see page 14), approximately
	Salt and freshly ground black pepper

GREMOLADA	1 garlic clove, very finely minced
	1 tablespoon minced lemon rind
	2 tablespoons chopped fresh parsley
	1 or 2 anchovy fillets, finely chopped (optional)

1. Preheat oven to 350°F.

2. Use a heavy broad casserole, 8- to 10-quart size, large enough to hold all the veal pieces flat-side down in one layer (or use 2 casseroles, but do not stack shank pieces on top of one another). Heat the butter over moderate heat. When it begins to foam, add the pancetta, onion, carrot, and celery, and sauté for about 5 minutes, until the carrot and celery begin to soften.

3. Dredge each piece of veal shank with flour, brushing off the excess. Heat the oil until it is very hot in a large skillet over moderate-high heat and place the floured shanks in the pan. Turn the shanks until they are browned on all sides, then place them flat-side down in the casserole with the pancetta and vegetables.

4. Skim all but about 1 tablespoon fat from the skillet. Pour in the wine and boil for 2 to 3 minutes while scraping the sides and bottom of the pan with a wooden spoon. Pour the wine and the deglazing over the veal shanks in the casserole.

5. Add the tomatoes, thyme, bay leaf, and parsley to the casserole with enough meat broth so that the liquid just covers the veal shanks. Add salt and pepper to taste. Turn the heat to moderate. When the broth begins to simmer, cover the casserole and place it in the preheated oven. Cook for 2 to 3 hours. Every ½ hour baste the veal shanks to keep them moist.

6. Just before serving, make the *gremolada:* Combine the garlic, lemon rind, parsley, and anchovy.

7. To serve, remove veal shanks from the casserole and place on individual plates. Cut the strings. Spoon some of the sauce over each piece of shank and top each serving with a sprinkling of *gremolada.*

Serves 6

NOTES: Each shank piece should be tied with string to prevent the meat from falling away from the bone and into the broth. When the veal shanks have finished cooking, the sauce around them should be rich and thick. If it is thin and watery, remove the pieces of veal and place the uncovered casserole over moderate-high heat on the stove. Cook until the sauce has thickened, stirring frequently so that it doesn't stick or burn on the bottom.

Ossobuco can be eaten as soon as it is taken from the oven. However, as with so many stews, it improves with a day's wait.

When preparing Risotto alla Milanese (see page 26) to serve with *ossobuco,* increase the quantity of rice to 2 cups and refer to the quantity chart on page 23.

Veal & Fresh Fennel

RISOTTO
CON VITELLO E FINOCCHIO

Fresh fennel adds its distinctive but subtle anise flavor and a delicate green color to this risotto of sliced veal. It makes a complete light supper when served before a salad of crisp watercress and sliced sweet pepper.

CONDIMENTI	2 tablespoons unsalted butter
	1 garlic clove, finely minced
	4 to 6 ounces veal scallops, sliced into thin julienne strips
	Salt and freshly ground black pepper
	1 cup chopped fresh fennel bulb
	½ cup light cream
	⅓ cup grated Parmesan cheese
	1 tablespoon chopped fresh parsley
BRODO	5 cups Basic Broth (see page 14), approximately
	½ cup dry white wine or broth
SOFFRITTO	2 tablespoons unsalted butter
	1 tablespoon oil
	⅓ cup finely minced onion
RISO	1½ cups Arborio rice

1. *CONDIMENTI:* Heat the butter in a small skillet over moderate heat. When it begins to foam, add the garlic and veal and cook for about 3 minutes, until the veal loses its pink color. Add salt and pepper to taste. Turn off the heat and set aside. Place the fennel in a small saucepan with water to cover and bring to a boil. Cook for 20 minutes, until the fennel is tender. Drain. Put the fennel in a food processor or blender with cream and purée. Set aside.

2. *BRODO:* Bring the broth to a steady simmer in a saucepan on top of the stove.

3. *SOFFRITTO:* Heat the butter and oil in a heavy 4-quart casserole over moderate heat. Add the onion and sauté for 1 to 2 minutes, until it begins to soften, being careful not to brown it.

4. *RISO:* Add the rice to the soffritto; using a wooden spoon, stir for 1 minute, making sure all the grains are well coated. Add the wine and stir until it is completely absorbed. Begin to add the simmering broth, ½ cup at a time, stirring frequently. Wait until each addition is almost completely absorbed before adding the next ½ cup, reserving about ¼ cup to add at the end. Stir frequently to prevent sticking.

5. After approximately 18 minutes, when the rice is tender but still firm, add the reserved broth and the condimenti—veal, fennel purée, Parmesan, and parsley—and stir vigorously to combine with the rice. Serve immediately.

Serves 4

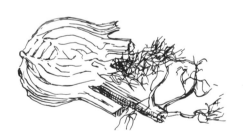

Meat & Tomato Sauce

RISOTTO
ALLA BOLOGNESE

An Italian classic, Bolognese sauce is traditionally made with a combination of finely chopped or ground veal, beef, and pork, gently simmered with tomatoes, wine, and other flavorings. We've simplified this sauce so that you can prepare it while you are cooking the risotto (you can also prepare it in advance and reheat it as you cook the risotto). We like to stir the Bolognese sauce into the risotto, but you can also treat it like the sauce that it is and serve it on top.

CONDIMENTI
- 1 tablespoon unsalted butter
- 1 tablespoon olive oil
- 3 tablespoons finely minced onion
- 2 tablespoons finely minced carrot
- 2 tablespoons finely minced celery
- ½ pound ground lean meat (beef, pork, or veal, or a combination)
- ½ cup dry white wine
- 1 tablespoon light cream
- 1 cup chopped canned Italian plum tomatoes, with their juice
- Pinch of grated nutmeg
- Salt and freshly ground black pepper
- ⅓ cup grated Parmesan cheese
- 1 tablespoon chopped fresh parsley

BRODO	5 cups Basic Broth (see page 14), approximately
	½ cup dry white wine or broth
SOFFRITTO	2 tablespoons unsalted butter
	1 tablespoon oil
	⅓ cup finely minced onion
RISO	1½ cups Arborio rice

1. CONDIMENTI: Heat the butter and oil in a 1½-quart heavy saucepan over moderate heat. When the butter begins to foam, add the onion, carrot, and celery and cook for 3 to 5 minutes, until the vegetables begin to soften. Add the meat and stir with a fork until all the meat has lost its pink color and begins to brown. Immediately add the wine, turn the heat to high, and cook until the wine is completely evaporated. Return the heat to moderate, add the cream, and cook for 2 to 3 minutes more. Add the tomatoes, nutmeg, and salt and pepper to taste. Turn the heat to low, and continue cooking the sauce while you prepare the risotto. Stir occasionally.

2. BRODO: Bring the broth to a steady simmer in a saucepan on top of the stove.

3. SOFFRITTO: Heat the butter and oil in a heavy 4-quart casserole over moderate heat. Add the onion and sauté for 1 to 2 minutes, until it begins to soften, being careful not to brown it.

4. RISO: Add the rice to the soffritto; using a wooden spoon, stir for 1 minute, making sure all the grains are well coated. Add the wine and stir until it is completely absorbed. Begin to add the simmering broth, ½ cup at a time, stirring frequently. Wait until each addition is almost completely absorbed before adding the next ½ cup, reserving about ¼ cup to add at the end. Stir frequently to prevent sticking.

5. After approximately 18 minutes, when the rice is tender but still firm, add the reserved broth and the condimenti—Bolognese sauce, Parmesan, and parsley—and stir vigorously to combine with the rice. Serve immediately.

Serves 4

Roast Beef

RISOTTO
ALLA FIORENTINA

This traditional risotto from the region around Florence is always served as an accompaniment to roast beef. After the roast is taken from the oven, the juices of the roast that accumulate in the pan are added as a flavoring to the cooking rice. The finished sirloin or standing rib roast should be allowed to stand for at least 15 minutes after it is taken from the oven, and that's the perfect length of time in which to make this simple delicious risotto. Serve with a big red wine such as Barolo.

BRODO	5 cups Basic Broth (see page 14), approximately
SOFFRITTO	2 tablespoons unsalted butter
	1 tablespoon oil
	⅓ cup finely minced onion
RISO	1½ cups Arborio rice

CONDIMENTI	1 cup juices from a roast of beef
	1 tablespoon unsalted butter
	⅓ cup grated Parmesan cheese
	1 tablespoon chopped fresh parsley

1. BRODO: Bring the broth to a steady simmer in a saucepan on top of the stove.

2. SOFFRITTO: Heat the butter and oil in a heavy 4-quart casserole over moderate heat. Add the onion and sauté for 1 to 2 minutes, until it begins to soften, being careful not to brown it.

3. RISO: Add the rice to the soffritto; using a wooden spoon, stir for 1 minute, making sure all the grains are well coated.

4. CONDIMENTI: Add the juices from the roast beef to the rice, and stir until they are completely absorbed. Begin to add the simmering broth, ½ cup at a time, stirring frequently. Wait until each addition is almost completely absorbed before adding the next ½ cup, reserving about ¼ cup to add at the end. Stir frequently to prevent sticking.

5. After approximately 18 minutes, when the rice is tender but still firm, add the reserved broth. Turn off the heat and immediately add the butter, Parmesan, and parsley, and stir vigorously to combine with the rice. Serve immediately.

Serves 4

VARIATION

To the soffritto add 2 tablespoons finely minced carrot, 2 tablespoons finely minced celery, and approximately 3 ounces sausage meat (1 sausage, out of its casing).

Lamb with *Egg* & *Lemon Sauce*

RISOTTO
ALL'AGNELLO CON UOVO E LIMONE

Baby lamb is the traditional Italian dish to serve on Easter Sunday. This risotto with tender young lamb in a flavorful egg and lemon sauce would grace any holiday table. The cooking time for the lamb is brief, so we recommend using the most tender lamb loin. You can also use meat cut from the leg or shoulder, but in that case you should increase the cooking time by about 10 minutes.

CONDIMENTI	1 tablespoon unsalted butter
	1 tablespoon vegetable oil
	2 tablespoons chopped onion
	2 tablespoons chopped prosciutto
	6 to 8 ounces lamb loin, cut into thin strips (about ¾ cup)
	Salt and freshly ground black pepper
	¾ cup dry white wine
	1 egg yolk
	2 tablespoons fresh lemon juice
	1 tablespoon chopped fresh marjoram, or 1 teaspoon dried
	2 tablespoons chopped fresh parsley
BRODO	6 cups Basic Broth (see page 14), approximately
	½ cup dry white wine or broth

SOFFRITTO	2 tablespoons unsalted butter
	1 tablespoon oil
	⅓ cup finely minced onion
RISO	1½ cups Arborio rice

1. CONDIMENTI: Heat the butter and oil in a large skillet over moderate heat; add the onion and prosciutto and cook for 1 to 2 minutes, until the onion begins to soften. Add the lamb and cook for 3 to 5 minutes, until the strips of meat are browned all over. Season with salt and pepper and add the wine. Turn the heat to moderate-high and cook for 2 to 3 minutes, until the wine is completely evaporated. Turn the heat to low, add just enough broth to cover the lamb, put lid on, and gently simmer while you prepare the risotto. Add more broth to the lamb if it begins to stick to the pan. In a small bowl, combine egg yolk, lemon juice, marjoram, and parsley and set aside.

2. BRODO: Bring the broth to a steady simmer in a saucepan on top of the stove.

3. SOFFRITTO: Heat the butter and oil in a heavy 4-quart casserole over moderate heat. Add the onion and sauté for 1 to 2 minutes, until it begins to soften, being careful not to brown it.

4. RISO: Add the rice to the soffritto; using a wooden spoon, stir for 1 minute, making sure all the grains are well coated. Add the wine and stir until it is completely absorbed. Begin to add the simmering broth, ½ cup at a time, stirring frequently. Wait until each addition is almost completely absorbed before adding the next ½ cup, reserving about ¼ cup to add at the end. Stir frequently to prevent sticking.

5. After approximately 18 minutes, when the rice is tender but still firm, add the reserved broth. Turn off heat and add remaining condimenti—lamb, the egg and lemon mixture—and stir well to incorporate all the ingredients. Serve immediately.

Serves 4

VARIATION

Omit the prosciutto and onion in step 1. Replace with 2 scallions, finely sliced, and ½ head of Boston lettuce, finely shredded. Add the lettuce to the sautéed scallions and cook until wilted. Add dill in place of the marjoram in step 5.

Lamb Stew

RISOTTO
CON SPEZZATINO DI AGNELLO

This richly seasoned lamb stew, cooked with prosciutto and wine until it is tender and very flavorful, is traditionally served together with Risotto al Vino Bianco (see Index). The finished risotto is molded into a ring shape with the lamb stew spooned into the center. First prepare the lamb as follows, and while it is cooking, prepare the risotto. Serve the two together as a main course.

2 tablespoons unsalted butter
1 tablespoon oil
⅓ cup finely minced onion

2 tablespoons chopped prosciutto
3 pounds lamb, shoulder or leg, cut into 1-inch cubes
1 cup dry white wine or broth
2 tablespoons tomato paste
½ cup chopped fresh basil
Risotto al Vino Bianco (see page 292), made with a
    double quantity of ingredients

1. Heat the butter and oil in a 4-quart heavy casserole; add the onion and prosciutto and cook until the onion begins to turn golden.

2. Add the lamb and continue cooking for 3 to 5 minutes, until the pieces are browned all over.

3. Add the wine, turn the heat to high, and boil vigorously until the wine is almost completely evaporated.

4. Return the heat to moderate, add the tomato paste, and stir well to coat the lamb. Add just enough water to cover the lamb. Place a lid on the casserole and cook for about 30 minutes, until the lamb is tender and the sauce around it has thickened. (The lamb can be prepared in advance up to this point. Reheat it while the risotto is cooking.)

5. Prepare the risotto. When it is finished cooking, spoon it into a chilled, buttered 10-inch ring mold. Let it stand for 2 to 3 minutes. Place a serving platter, top side down, over the mold, then turn over mold and plate together so that the mold is resting on top of the platter. Ease the mold off the risotto.

6. Pour the lamb into the center of the ring of risotto, and garnish with basil.

To serve, spoon some risotto on each plate with a portion of the lamb alongside it.

Serves 8

Calf's Liver & Onions

RISOTTO
CON FEGATO ALLA VENEZIANA

One of the legendary foods of Venice is sautéed calf's liver and onions served with polenta. We took the liberty of substituting Risotto al Parmigiano for the polenta, and the results convinced us that this too deserves to be a culinary classic. The risotto and the liver and onions are prepared side by side. The liver will cook in under a minute, so prepare the onions but wait to cook the liver until the risotto is almost finished.

3 tablespoons vegetable oil
2 cups thinly sliced onions
8 ounces calf's liver,
   cut into ¼-inch-thick slices
Salt and freshly ground black pepper
Risotto al Parmigiano (see page 53)

1. Heat the vegetable oil in a skillet over moderate heat. Add the onions and cook for about 5 minutes, until they begin to soften. Turn the heat to low and continue cooking, stirring occasionally, for about 10 minutes, until the onions are golden and begin to turn brown.

2. Meanwhile, trim away the outer membrane of the liver and cut the slices into ½-inch-wide strips.

3. When you have added all but the last addition of broth to the risotto, turn the heat under the onions to moderate. When onions begin to sizzle slightly, add the liver, salt and pepper to taste, and cook, stirring, just until the pieces of meat become browned on the outside but are still pink inside. Serve immediately with the risotto.

Serves 4

NOTE: Pale pink baby calf's liver is preferable; the redder the liver, the older the calf. Have the liver cut into ¼-inch-thick slices.

Veal Kidney with Garlic, Oil, & Parsley

RISOTTO
AI ROGNONCINI TRIFOLATI

This is our adaptation of a classic Milanese risotto. The kidney is prepared *trifolati* style: very thinly sliced, cooked in olive oil and garlic, and sprinkled with a generous helping of fresh parsley. In Milan, the sautéed kidneys are served over Risotto alla Milanese (see Index), but we found the flavors are better when combined. For this risotto, use only a veal kidney; beef kidney has too strong a flavor, and lamb not enough. This risotto made converts of our friends who insisted they didn't like kidneys.

CONDIMENTI	1 veal kidney, about 6–8 ounces
	2 tablespoons olive oil
	1 large garlic clove, finely minced

¼ cup chopped fresh parsley

⅓ cup grated Parmesan cheese

BRODO | 5 cups Basic Broth (see page 14), approximately

½ cup dry white wine or broth

SOFFRITTO | 2 tablespoons unsalted butter

1 tablespoon oil

⅓ cup finely minced onion

2 tablespoons finely minced carrot

2 tablespoons finely minced celery

RISO | 1½ cups Arborio rice

¼ teaspoon powdered saffron

1. CONDIMENTI: Soak the kidney in cold water for 1 hour before you plan to cook it; cut out the white membrane and slice the kidney crosswise as thinly as possible. Heat the oil in a small skillet over moderate heat, add the garlic and the sliced kidney, and cook for about 5 minutes, while stirring, until the kidney begins to turn brown. Turn off the heat. Stir in the parsley and set aside.

2. BRODO: Bring the broth to a steady simmer in a saucepan on top of the stove.

3. SOFFRITTO: Heat the butter and oil in a heavy 4-quart casserole over moderate heat. Add the onion, carrot, and celery and sauté for

1 to 2 minutes, until the onion begins to soften, being careful not to brown it.

4. *RISO:* Add the rice to the soffritto; using a wooden spoon, stir for 1 minute, making sure all the grains are well coated. Add the saffron. Pour in the wine and stir until it is completely absorbed. Begin to add the simmering broth, ½ cup at a time, stirring frequently. Wait until each addition is almost completely absorbed before adding the next ½ cup, reserving about ¼ cup to add at the end. Stir frequently to prevent sticking.

5. After approximately 18 minutes, when the rice is tender but still firm, add the reserved broth and the condimenti—the kidney and Parmesan—and stir vigorously to combine with the rice. Serve immediately.

Serves 4

Sweetbreads

RISOTTO CON LE ANIMELLE

With their gentle flavor and texture, sweetbreads are one of the great culinary delicacies. In this risotto, Marsala adds its rich flavor to the rice and sweetbreads to make this a first-class main course.

CONDIMENTI	8 to 10 ounces sweetbreads
	1 teaspoon salt
	¼ cup lemon juice

Salt and freshly ground black pepper

4 tablespoons unsalted butter

½ cup dry Marsala wine

⅓ cup grated Parmesan cheese

BRODO	5 cups Basic Broth (see page 14), approximately
	½ cup dry Marsala wine

SOFFRITTO	2 tablespoons unsalted butter
	2 ounces prosciutto, cut into slivers

RISO	1½ cups Arborio rice

1. CONDIMENTI: Place the sweetbreads in a large saucepan with the salt, lemon juice, and enough cold water to cover. Bring to a boil and simmer for 10 minutes. Plunge the sweetbreads into a bowl of cold water and allow to cool. Drain well, pat dry, and peel away and discard the membranes and any connective tissue. Cut the sweetbreads into ½-inch-thick slices and season with salt and pepper. Heat 2 tablespoons of butter in a small skillet over moderate-high heat. When the butter begins to foam, add the sweetbreads and cook for 6 to 7 minutes, turning them once, carefully. Cook for another 5 to 6 minutes. Add ½ cup Marsala and continue cooking until the wine is almost evaporated. Cover to keep warm and set aside.

2. BRODO: Bring the broth to a steady simmer in a saucepan on top of the stove.

3. SOFFRITTO: Heat the butter in a heavy 4-quart casserole over moderate heat. Add the prosciutto and sauté for 1 to 2 minutes.

4. RISO: Add the rice to the soffritto; using a wooden spoon, stir for 1 minute, making sure all the grains are well coated. Add remaining ½ cup Marsala and stir until it is almost completely absorbed. Begin to add the simmering broth, ½ cup at a time, stirring frequently. Wait until each addition is almost completely absorbed before adding the next ½ cup, reserving about ¼ cup to add at the end. Stir frequently to prevent sticking.

5. After approximately 18 minutes, when the rice is tender but still firm, add the reserved broth. Turn off the heat and add the condimenti—the remaining butter and Parmesan—and stir vigorously to combine with the rice. Serve immediately with a portion of sweetbreads on top of each serving.

Serves 4

Tripe

RISOTTO
CON LA TRIPPA ALLA VENETA

Tripe is a favorite Italian food, which remains largely unappreciated in this country. A flavorful risotto with tripe is a perfect way to become acquainted with this specialty. Serve with a bold red wine, such as Spanna or Gattinara.

CONDIMENTI	10 to 12 ounces precooked honeycomb tripe (available from most butchers and many supermarkets)
	1 onion, peeled and left whole
	1 carrot, scraped
	1 celery rib
	1 tablespoon salt
	⅓ cup grated Parmesan cheese
BRODO	5½ cups Basic Broth (see page 14), approximately
SOFFRITTO	3 tablespoons oil
	2 ounces pancetta, finely chopped
	⅓ cup finely minced onion
	2 tablespoons finely minced celery
	2 small tomatoes, peeled, seeded, and chopped, or ½ cup canned Italian tomatoes, well drained and chopped
	1 teaspoon fresh rosemary, or ¼ teaspoon dried
RISO	1½ cups Arborio rice

1. CONDIMENTI: Place the tripe with enough cold water to cover in a large saucepan over high heat. Add the onion, carrot, celery, and salt and bring to a boil. Simmer for 1 hour. Remove the tripe from the liquid and slice into ½-inch-thick strips.

2. BRODO: Bring the broth to a steady simmer in a saucepan on top of the stove.

3. SOFFRITTO: Heat the oil in a heavy 4-quart casserole over moderate heat. Add the pancetta, onion, celery, tomatoes, and rosemary, and sauté for 3 to 5 minutes, until the onion begins to soften, being careful not to brown it.

4. RISO: Add the rice to the soffritto; using a wooden spoon, stir for 1 minute, making sure all the grains are well coated. Add ½ cup of the simmering broth and the sliced tripe and stir until the liquid is almost completely absorbed. Continue to add the simmering broth, ½ cup at a time, stirring frequently. Wait until each addition is almost completely absorbed before adding the next ½ cup, reserving about ¼ cup to add at the end. Stir frequently to prevent sticking.

5. After approximately 18 minutes, when the rice is tender but still firm, add the reserved broth. Turn off the heat and add the remaining condimenti—Parmesan—and stir vigorously to combine with the rice. Serve immediately.

Serves 4

Chicken, Mushrooms, & Pine Nuts

RISOTTO
CON POLLO, FUNGHI E PIGNOLI

The earthy taste of the shiitake mushrooms provides the essential character for this risotto. Use only the mushroom caps and slice them into thin strips. Pine nuts on each serving lend a nice crunch to this creamy dish. Serve as a main course with lightly steamed broccoli, which has been cooled and dressed with lemon and oil.

CONDIMENTI	2 tablespoons unsalted butter
	1 garlic clove, finely minced
	1 whole boneless chicken breast, about ½ pound, skin and cartilage removed, and diced
	4 ounces wild mushrooms (shiitake, oyster, or other), stems removed, sliced (about 2 cups)
	½ cup light cream
	Salt and freshly ground black pepper

4 tablespoons pine nuts

⅓ cup grated Parmesan cheese

1 tablespoon chopped fresh parsley

BRODO	5 cups Basic Broth (see page 14), approximately
	½ cup dry white wine or broth

SOFFRITTO	2 tablespoons unsalted butter
	1 tablespoon oil
	2 tablespoons finely minced onion

RISO	1½ cups Arborio rice

1. *CONDIMENTI:* Heat 1 tablespoon of the butter with the garlic in a skillet over moderate heat. When the butter begins to foam, add the chicken pieces and cook for 5 minutes, until they turn opaque. Add the mushrooms and cook, stirring occasionally, for about 5 minutes longer, until the mushrooms are tender. Add the cream and salt and pepper to taste, and simmer for 3 to 5 minutes longer, until the cream has thickened slightly. Turn off the heat and set aside. In a separate small skillet over moderate heat, melt remaining tablespoon of butter. Add pine nuts, and sauté gently until they turn golden brown. Turn off heat and set aside.

2. *BRODO:* Bring the broth to a steady simmer in a saucepan on top of the stove.

3. *SOFFRITTO:* Heat the butter and oil in a heavy 4-quart casserole over moderate heat. Add the onion and sauté for 1 to 2 minutes, until it begins to soften, being careful not to brown it.

4. *RISO:* Add the rice to the soffritto; using a wooden spoon, stir for 1 minute, making sure all the grains are well coated. Add the wine and stir until it is completely absorbed. Begin to add the simmering broth, ½ cup at a time, stirring frequently. Wait until each addition is almost completely absorbed before adding the next ½ cup. Stir frequently to prevent sticking.

5. After approximately 18 minutes, when the rice is tender but still firm, add the reserved broth and the condimenti—the chicken-mushroom-cream mixture, Parmesan, and parsley—and stir vigorously to combine with the rice. Serve immediately. Sprinkle pine nuts on each portion.

Serves 4

VARIATIONS

1. In place of the shiitake mushrooms, substitute 8 ounces cultivated white mushrooms, caps only, or ⅓ ounce dried porcini mushrooms, which have been soaked in hot water for 30 minutes, drained, and coarsely chopped.

2. In place of pine nuts use slivered almonds.

Chicken, Prosciutto, & Tomato

RISOTTO
CON POLLO, PROSCIUTTO E POMODORI

The prosciutto and tomatoes add a hearty flavor to the chicken. We serve this risotto as a second course after a warm salad of julienne carrots and zucchini that are lightly steamed and dressed with a dash of fresh lemon juice and oil.

CONDIMENTI	2 tablespoons olive oil
	2 tablespoons finely minced onion
	1 boneless chicken breast, about ½ pound, skin and cartilage removed, cut into 1-inch pieces
	3 ounces prosciutto, diced (about ½ cup)
	2 small tomatoes, peeled, seeded, and chopped, or ½ cup canned Italian tomatoes, well drained and chopped
	1 tablespoon chopped fresh parsley
	¼ cup grated Parmesan cheese
BRODO	5 cups Basic Broth (see page 14), approximately
	½ cup dry white wine or broth
SOFFRITTO	2 tablespoons unsalted butter
	1 tablespoon oil
	⅓ cup finely minced onion
RISO	1½ cups Arborio rice

1. CONDIMENTI: Heat the oil in a skillet over moderate heat; add the onion and sauté for 1 to 2 minutes, until the onion begins to soften. Add the chicken, prosciutto, and tomatoes and continue cooking, stirring frequently, for about 10 minutes, until the chicken pieces are tender. Turn off the heat and set aside.

2. BRODO: Bring the broth to a steady simmer in a saucepan on top of the stove.

3. SOFFRITTO: Heat the butter and oil in a heavy 4-quart casserole over moderate heat. Add the onion and sauté for 1 to 2 minutes,

until it begins to soften, being careful not to brown it.

4. RISO: Add the rice to the soffritto; using a wooden spoon, stir for 1 minute, making sure all the grains are well coated. Add the wine and stir until it is completely absorbed. Begin to add the simmering broth, ½ cup at a time, stirring frequently. Wait until each addition is almost completely absorbed before adding the next ½ cup, reserving about ¼ to add at the end. Stir frequently to prevent sticking.

5. After approximately 18 minutes, when the rice is tender but still firm, add the reserved broth and the condimenti—the chicken, tomatoes, and parsley. Turn off the heat and immediately add the Parmesan and stir vigorously to combine with the rice. Serve immediately.

Serves 4

Chicken & Watercress

RISOTTO
CON POLLO E CRESCIONE

The lush green purée of watercress, shallots, and herbs combines with the chicken to create a refreshing and tangy taste. This rich risotto can be a main course for elegant warm-weather dinners. Serve with a chilled crisp white wine, such as Orvieto or Pinot Grigio.

CONDIMENTI	2 tablespoons unsalted butter
	1 boneless chicken breast, about ½ pound, skin and cartilage removed, sliced into thin strips

Salt and freshly ground black pepper

3 tablespoons finely minced shallot

1 cup dry white wine

1 small bunch of watercress

1 tablespoon lemon juice

2 tablespoons snipped fresh chives, or 1 teaspoon dried

½ cup light cream

BRODO	5 cups Basic Broth (see page 14), approximately
	½ cup dry white wine or broth

SOFFRITTO	2 tablespoons unsalted butter
	1 tablespoon oil
	⅓ cup finely minced onion

RISO	1½ cups Arborio rice

1. CONDIMENTI: Heat the butter in a skillet over moderate heat.
When it begins to foam, add the chicken and sauté for about 5 minutes,
until the meat is tender and cooked through. Add salt and pepper to
taste. Remove the chicken from pan and reserve. Add the shallot and
wine to the same pan, turn the heat to moderate-high, and boil vigor-

ously until the wine has been reduced to about ¼ cup. Meanwhile, wash the watercress, drop it into boiling salted water for 30 seconds, and drain it well. In a food processor or blender, combine the watercress, shallot and wine reduction, lemon juice, and chives, and reduce to a purée. Set aside.

2. BRODO: Bring the broth to a steady simmer in a saucepan on top of the stove.

3. SOFFRITTO: Heat the butter and oil in a heavy 4-quart casserole over moderate heat. Add the onion and sauté for 1 to 2 minutes, until it begins to soften, being careful not to brown it.

4. RISO: Add the rice to the soffritto; using a wooden spoon, stir for 1 minute, making sure all the grains are well coated. Add the wine and stir until it is completely absorbed. Begin to add the simmering broth, ½ cup at a time, stirring frequently. Wait until each addition is almost completely absorbed before adding the next ½ cup. Stir frequently to prevent sticking.

5. After approximately 18 minutes, when the rice is tender but still firm, add the condimenti—sautéed chicken, watercress purée, and cream—and stir vigorously to combine with the rice. Serve immediately.

Serves 4

Chicken with Olives

RISOTTO
POLLO ALLA PROVENZALE

The black olives, red tomatoes, and sweet yellow pepper give this dish a Mediterranean flavor as well as a colorful appearance. Serve this risotto before an entrée of grilled fresh tuna or swordfish and a crisp green salad.

CONDIMENTI	1 tablespoon olive oil
	2 tablespoons unsalted butter
	1 garlic clove, finely minced
	½ yellow pepper, seeds and core removed, cut into thin strips
	½ cup pitted black olives, coarsely chopped
	1 boneless chicken breast, about ½ pound, skin and cartilage removed, cut into thin strips
	1 cup crushed or finely chopped canned Italian plum tomatoes, with their juice
BRODO	5 cups Basic Broth (see page 14), approximately
	½ cup dry white wine or broth
SOFFRITTO	2 tablespoons unsalted butter
	1 tablespoon oil
	⅓ cup finely minced onion
RISO	1½ cups Arborio rice

1. CONDIMENTI: Heat the oil and butter in a skillet over moderate heat. Add the garlic, yellow pepper, and olives and cook for 5 minutes. Stir in the chicken and tomatoes. Turn the heat to low and simmer slowly while you prepare the risotto, stirring occasionally.

2. BRODO: Bring the broth to a steady simmer in a saucepan on top of the stove.

3. SOFFRITTO: Heat the butter and oil in a heavy 4-quart casserole over moderate heat. Add the onion and sauté for 1 to 2 minutes, until it begins to soften, being careful not to brown it.

4. RISO: Add the rice to the soffritto; using a wooden spoon, stir for 1 minute, making sure all the grains are well coated. Add the wine and stir until it is completely absorbed. Begin to add the simmering broth, ½ cup at a time, stirring frequently. Wait until each addition is almost completely absorbed before adding the next ½ cup, reserving about ¼ cup to add at the end. Stir frequently to prevent sticking.

5. After approximately 18 minutes, when the rice is tender but still firm, add the reserved broth and the condimenti—the chicken-tomatoes-olive mixture—and stir vigorously to combine with the rice. Serve immediately.

Serves 4

VARIATIONS

1. Add 1 tablespoon balsamic vinegar to the chicken with the garlic, pepper, and olives.

2. Prepare recipe, but reserve the yellow pepper. While the risotto is cooking, wash the pepper and place it directly over a low flame on the stove or under the oven broiler, turning frequently until the pepper skin has been completely blackened. Run the pepper under cold water to remove the charred skin, cut it into halves, and remove the stem, ribs, and seeds. Slice the pepper into strips and spoon 2 tablespoons of olive oil over them. Serve the risotto with yellow pepper strips as a garnish on each serving.

Turkey & Leeks

RISOTTO
CON TACCHINO E PORRI

Turkey is just beginning to become established in the culinary mainstream as a replacement for veal in traditional Italian recipes. Here it makes the move to risotto with great success. What delights us most about this dish is how the subtle flavors of the Marsala, sage, and leeks gently emerge and are discovered in each bite. We call for uncooked turkey, but you can also use leftover turkey.

CONDIMENTI	2 tablespoons unsalted butter
	½ pound boneless turkey breast or turkey cutlets, cut into thin strips (about 1 cup)
	2 medium-size leeks, white parts only, washed thoroughly and cut lengthwise into julienne strips
	½ cup dry Marsala wine
	¾ cup light cream
	½ teaspoon crushed dried sage
BRODO	5½ cups Basic Broth (see page 14), approximately
SOFFRITTO	2 tablespoons unsalted butter
	1 tablespoon oil
	⅓ cup finely minced onion
RISO	1½ cups Arborio rice

1. CONDIMENTI: Heat the butter in a skillet over moderate heat. When it begins to foam, add the turkey and cook for 5 minutes, stirring occasionally. Add the leeks and continue cooking until they are softened. Pour in the Marsala, turn the heat to moderate-high, and boil vigorously until it is reduced to about a tablespoon. Add the cream and sage. Turn the heat to low and simmer slowly for 15 to 18 minutes while the risotto is cooking.

2. BRODO: Bring the broth to a steady simmer in a saucepan on top of the stove.

3. SOFFRITTO: Heat the butter and oil in a heavy 4-quart casserole over moderate heat. Add the onion and sauté for 1 to 2 minutes, until it begins to soften, being careful not to brown it.

4. RISO: Add the rice to the soffritto; using a wooden spoon, stir for 1 minute, making sure all the grains are well coated. Begin to add the simmering broth, ½ cup at a time, stirring frequently. Wait until each addition is almost completely absorbed before adding the next ½ cup. Stir frequently to prevent sticking.

5. After approximately 18 minutes, when the rice is tender but still firm, add the condimenti—the turkey-leeks-cream mixture—and stir vigorously to combine with the rice. Serve immediately.

Serves 4

VARIATIONS

1. Add 2 tablespoons chopped prosciutto to the soffritto.

2. Omit the Marsala from the condimenti and add it to the rice before adding any broth. This will give more Marsala flavor to the risotto.

Turkey, Red Peppers, & Tomatoes

RISOTTO
ROSSO AL TACCHINO

The taste of the turkey is brought to new heights with the addition of tomatoes and sweet red pepper. Serve this as a main course after an antipasto of steamed fresh fennel bulb dressed with extra-virgin olive oil, lemon juice, and freshly ground black pepper.

CONDIMENTI

2 tablespoons unsalted butter

½ pound boneless breast of turkey or turkey cutlets, cut into ¼-inch strips about 2 inches long

½ medium-size sweet red bell pepper, seeded and cut into thin strips

Salt and freshly ground black pepper

1 tablespoon finely minced shallot (if not available use scallion, white part only)

1 garlic clove, finely minced

1 small tomato, peeled, seeded, and chopped (¼ cup)

1 teaspoon dried thyme

½ cup dry Marsala wine

⅓ cup grated Parmesan cheese

BRODO	5½ cups Basic Broth (see page 14), approximately

SOFFRITTO	2 tablespoons unsalted butter
	1 tablespoon oil
	⅓ cup finely minced onion

RISO	1½ cups Arborio rice

1. CONDIMENTI: Heat the butter in a skillet over moderate heat. When it begins to foam, add the turkey strips and red pepper, and salt and pepper to taste. Sauté for 3 to 5 minutes, until the turkey begins to turn golden. Add the shallot, garlic, tomato, and thyme and continue cooking for 2 to 3 minutes longer. Add the Marsala, turn the heat to moderate-high, and boil vigorously until the liquid is reduced to about half. Turn off heat and set aside.

2. BRODO: Bring the broth to a steady simmer in a saucepan on top of the stove.

3. SOFFRITTO: Heat the butter and oil in a heavy 4-quart casserole over moderate heat. Add the onion and sauté for 1 to 2 minutes, until it begins to soften, being careful not to brown it.

4. RISO: Add the rice to the soffritto; using a wooden spoon, stir for 1 minute, making sure all the grains are well coated. Begin to add the simmering broth, ½ cup at a time, stirring frequently. Wait until each addition is almost completely absorbed before adding the next ½ cup, reserving about ¼ cup to add at the end. Stir frequently to prevent sticking.

5. After approximately 18 minutes, when the rice is tender but still firm, add the reserved broth and the condimenti—the turkey and red pepper mixture and the Parmesan—and stir vigorously to combine with the rice. Serve immediately.

Serves 4

Chicken Livers & Capers

RISOTTO
CON FEGATINI E CAPPERI

We adapted this recipe from the Tuscan *crostini di fegatini,* a flavorful antipasto made with a coarse tangy blend of chicken livers, capers, and sage—a combination we found irresistible for risotto. Serve as an entrée after a first course of barely cooked asparagus spears, gently coated with lemon butter.

CONDIMENTI

2 tablespoons unsalted butter

1 tablespoon olive oil

1 garlic clove, finely minced

1 tablespoon finely minced onion

2 tablespoons chopped prosciutto

¼ pound chicken livers, cut into small pieces

1 tablespoon capers

2 teaspoons crushed dried sage

½ cup Basic Broth (see page 14)

⅓ cup grated Parmesan cheese

BRODO	5 cups Basic Broth (see page 14), approximately
	½ cup dry white wine or broth

SOFFRITTO	2 tablespoons unsalted butter
	1 tablespoon oil
	⅓ cup finely minced onion

RISO	1½ cups Arborio rice

1. CONDIMENTI: Heat the butter with the oil in a skillet over moderate heat. When the butter begins to foam, add the garlic and onion and cook briefly until the garlic turns golden. Add the prosciutto, chicken livers, capers, and crushed sage and cook for 5 minutes. Add the ½ cup broth, turn the heat to moderate-high, and continue cooking until the broth is reduced to half. Turn off heat and set aside.

2. BRODO: Bring the 5 cups broth to a steady simmer in a saucepan on top of the stove.

3. SOFFRITTO: Heat the butter and oil in a heavy 4-quart casserole over moderate heat. Add the onion and sauté for 1 to 2 minutes, until it begins to soften, being careful not to brown it.

4. RISO: Add the rice to the soffritto; using a wooden spoon, stir for 1 minute, making sure all the grains are well coated. Add the wine and stir until it is completely absorbed. Begin to add the simmering broth, ½ cup at a time, stirring frequently. Wait until each addition is almost completely absorbed before adding the next ½ cup, reserving about ¼ cup to add at the end. Stir frequently to prevent sticking.

5. After approximately 18 minutes, when the rice is tender but still firm, add the reserved broth and the condimenti—the chicken liver-caper-sage mixture and Parmesan. Stir vigorously to combine with the rice. Serve immediately.

Serves 4

Chicken Livers & Marsala

RISOTTO
ALLA TRASTEVERINA

In this robust risotto, the wine and chicken livers are cooked together until the wine becomes thick, giving this dish an intense Marsala flavor. Serve as a main course with barely cooked fresh peas flecked with diced prosciutto.

CONDIMENTI	2 tablespoons unsalted butter
	4 ounces chicken livers (3 or 4 livers), cut into small pieces
	Salt and freshly ground black pepper
	½ cup dry Marsala wine
	¼ cup light cream
	⅓ cup grated Parmesan cheese
	1 tablespoon finely chopped fresh parsley
BRODO	5½ cups Basic Broth (see page 14), approximately
SOFFRITTO	2 tablespoons unsalted butter
	1 tablespoon oil
	⅓ cup finely minced onion
RISO	1½ cups Arborio rice

1. CONDIMENTI: Heat the butter in a small skillet over moderate heat. When it begins to foam, add the chicken livers, season with salt and pepper to taste, and gently sauté for 5 to 8 minutes, until the livers are cooked through. Add the Marsala and continue cooking until the liquid has been reduced to about half and has thickened. Turn off the heat and set aside.

2. BRODO: Bring the broth to a steady simmer in a saucepan on top of the stove.

3. SOFFRITTO: Heat the butter and oil in a heavy 4-quart casserole over moderate heat. Add the onion and sauté for 1 to 2 minutes, until it begins to soften, being careful not to brown it.

4. RISO: Add the rice to the soffritto; using a wooden spoon, stir for 1 minute, making sure all the grains are well coated. Begin to add the simmering broth, ½ cup at a time, stirring frequently. Wait until each addition is almost completely absorbed before adding the next ½ cup, reserving about ¼ cup to add at the end. Stir frequently to prevent sticking.

5. After approximately 18 minutes, when the rice is tender but still firm, add the reserved broth and the condimenti—chicken livers, cream, Parmesan, and parsley—and stir vigorously to combine with the rice. Serve immediately.

Serves 4

VARIATION

Add 2 tablespoons finely chopped pancetta to the chicken livers, and omit the cream in step 5.

Chicken Livers & Dried Porcini Mushrooms

RISOTTO
CON FEGATINI E PORCINI

The classic combination of chicken livers and rice is transformed into an unexpected savory delight with the addition of dried porcini and Marsala wine. This is a hearty main course for lunch or dinner; serve with salad of green and red lettuce, a warm loaf of crusty bread, and a big red wine, such as Barolo.

CONDIMENTI	⅓-ounce package dried porcini, approximately
	4 ounces chicken livers (3 or 4 livers), cut into small uniform pieces
	2 tablespoons unsalted butter
	⅓ cup grated Parmesan cheese
	1 tablespoon finely chopped fresh parsley
BRODO	4 cups Basic Broth (see page 14), approximately
	1 cup porcini liquid, strained
	½ cup dry Marsala wine
SOFFRITTO	2 tablespoons unsalted butter
	1 tablespoon oil
	⅓ cup finely minced onion
RISO	1½ cups Arborio rice

1. CONDIMENTI: Place the porcini in a small bowl with 1 cup boiling or very hot water and allow to stand for 30 minutes. Strain the liquid into a saucepan with the broth. Drain the porcini, coarsely chop, and set aside.

2. BRODO: Bring the broth with the porcini liquid to a steady simmer in a saucepan on top of the stove.

3. SOFFRITTO: Heat the butter and oil in a heavy 4-quart casserole over moderate heat. Add the onion and sauté for 1 to 2 minutes, until it begins to soften, being careful not to brown it.

4. RISO: Add the rice to the soffritto; using a wooden spoon, stir for 1 minute, making sure all the grains are well coated. Add the Marsala and stir until it is completely absorbed. Add the chicken livers and the porcini and begin to add the simmering broth, ½ cup at a time, stirring frequently. Wait until each addition is almost completely absorbed before adding the next ½ cup, reserving about ¼ cup to add at the end. Stir frequently to prevent sticking.

5. After approximately 18 minutes, when the rice is tender but still firm, add the reserved broth. Turn off the heat and immediately add the remaining condimenti—butter, Parmesan, and parsley—and stir vigorously to combine with the rice. Serve immediately.

Serves 4

VARIATIONS

1. Add dry white wine, Vermouth, or broth in place of Marsala.

2. If you want to use cultivated fresh mushrooms in place of dried porcini, use 1 cup coarsely chopped.

Goose Liver

RISOTTO
CON FEGATO D'OCA

This delicious risotto captures the richness of the fresh goose liver. This is an elegant opener to a dinner of grilled roasted veal. Serve with the Champagne used in the risotto preparation.

CONDIMENTI	2 tablespoons unsalted butter
	1 shallot, finely minced
	5 to 6 ounces fresh goose liver, cut into 1-inch pieces
	¼ cup light cream
	⅓ cup grated Parmesan cheese
	2 tablespoons chopped fresh parsley
BRODO	5 cups Basic Broth (see page 14), approximately
	½ cup sparkling dry white wine or Champagne
SOFFRITTO	2 tablespoons unsalted butter
	1 tablespoon oil
	⅓ cup finely minced onion
	1 garlic clove, finely minced
RISO	1½ cups Arborio rice

1. CONDIMENTI: Heat the butter in a small skillet over moderate heat and sauté the shallot for 2 minutes. Add the goose liver and continue cooking for 5 to 7 minutes, until the liver is cooked through. Place the liver and shallot in a food processor and process for 30 seconds, or chop fine with a knife. Set aside.

2. BRODO: Bring the broth to a steady simmer in a saucepan on top of the stove.

3. SOFFRITTO: Heat the butter and oil in a heavy 4-quart casserole over moderate heat. Add the onion and garlic and sauté for 1 to 2 minutes, until the onion begins to soften, being careful not to brown it.

4. RISO: Add the rice to the soffritto; using a wooden spoon, stir for 1 minute, making sure all the grains are well coated. Add the wine and stir until it is completely absorbed. Begin to add the simmering broth, ½ cup at a time, stirring frequently. Wait until each addition is almost completely absorbed before adding the next ½ cup, reserving about ¼ cup to add at the end. Stir frequently to prevent sticking.

5. After approximately 18 minutes, when the rice is tender but still firm, turn off the heat and immediately add the reserved broth and the condimenti—goose liver, cream, Parmesan, and parsley—and stir vigorously to combine with the rice. Serve immediately.

Serves 4

Quail

RISOTTO
CON LE QUAGLIE ALLA PIEMONTESE

This is an elegant main course of gently roasted quail, flavored with pancetta and rosemary and served on a bed of Basic Risotto. Top each serving of rice with two quail; it will be a show-stopper. Serve with a full-bodied red wine, such as Barbaresco.

4 ounces pancetta, diced
2 tablespoons unsalted butter
8 semi-boneless quail, innards removed and left whole
Salt and freshly ground black pepper
1 tablespoon chopped fresh rosemary, or 1 teaspoon dried
½ cup dry white wine
2 tablespoons chopped fresh parsley
Basic Recipe (see page 9)

1. Preheat oven to 425°F.

2. Place the pancetta in a shallow flameproof baking dish or roasting pan just large enough to hold all the quail in one layer. Over moderate heat, cook the pancetta until it has rendered most of its fat and begins to brown. Remove the pancetta from the dish to a separate bowl or saucepan to keep warm.

3. Add the butter to the baking dish with the pancetta fat. When it has melted, add the quail and carefully brown them on both sides. Season the quail with salt and pepper. Add the rosemary and white wine and place the baking dish in the oven.

4. When the quail have been roasting for 30 minutes, begin to prepare the risotto.

5. After approximately 18 minutes, when the rice is tender but still firm, take the quail from the oven and finish preparing the risotto.

6. Top each serving of risotto with 2 quail, a spoonful of juices from the roasting pan, and a tablespoon of browned pancetta. Garnish each serving with a sprinkling of fresh parsley.

Serves 4

Duck

RISOTTO ALL'ANATRA

This satisfying risotto captures the richness of the duck. It makes a good main course for a hearty midwinter dinner. Serve with a big red wine, such as Barolo or Amarone. Follow with a salad of endive, fresh fennel bulb, and tomatoes in a garlic vinaigrette.

CONDIMENTI   1 tablespoon unsalted butter

1 garlic clove, sliced

1 duck, 5 to 6 pounds, innards removed and cut into quarters (frozen duck should be defrosted and cut)

Salt and freshly ground black pepper

½ cup dry white wine

⅓-ounce package dried porcini, approximately

⅓ cup grated Parmesan cheese

BRODO	4½ cups Basic Broth (see page 14), approximately
	1 cup porcini liquid, strained

SOFFRITTO	3 tablespoons unsalted butter
	2 tablespoons finely minced onion

RISO	1½ cups Arborio rice

1. CONDIMENTI: Heat the butter in a 4-quart casserole over moderate heat. When it begins to foam, add the garlic and cook, for 1 minute, to flavor the butter. Remove the garlic from the pot. Add the duck to the butter, sprinkle with salt and pepper to taste, and sauté, while turning, until the pieces are browned on all sides. Add the wine, turn the heat to high, and cook until evaporated. Add 1½ cups water and bring to a boil. Turn the heat to moderate-low, cover the pot, and cook the duck for 45 minutes, or until it is tender and cooked through.

Meanwhile, place the dried porcini in a small bowl with 1 cup boiling or very hot water and allow to stand for 30 minutes. Strain the liquid into a saucepan with the broth, coarsely chop the porcini and set aside.

When the duck is tender, take it from the casserole, remove the skin and bones, and cut the meat into small pieces. Skim the fat from the juices in the pot, using a spoon. Return the meat to the casserole, add porcini, and continue cooking over low heat with the existing sauce while you prepare the risotto.

2. BRODO: Bring the broth with the strained porcini liquid to a steady simmer in a saucepan on top of the stove.

3. *SOFFRITTO:* Heat the butter in a heavy 4-quart casserole over moderate heat. Add the onion and sauté for 1 to 2 minutes, until it begins to soften, being careful not to brown it.

4. *RISO:* Add the rice to the soffritto; using a wooden spoon, stir for 1 minute, making sure all the grains are well coated. Begin to add the simmering broth, ½ cup at a time, stirring frequently. Wait until each addition is almost completely absorbed before adding the next ½ cup, reserving about ¼ cup to add at the end. Stir frequently to prevent sticking.

5. After approximately 18 minutes, when the rice is tender but still firm, add the reserved broth. Turn off the heat and add the remaining condimenti—Parmesan—and stir vigorously to combine with the rice. Turn the risotto out onto a preheated serving platter and spoon the duck and porcini with its sauce into the center. Serve immediately.

Serves 4

Spicy Rabbit

RISOTTO
AL CONIGLIO

The cool, rainy autumn weather of Northern Italy makes this hearty risotto of spicy rabbit a popular fall dish. Rabbit has a tender texture and delicate flavor that falls somewhere between chicken and veal. In this highly seasoned risotto, the rabbit is cooked twice, first in the oven until it is falling-off-the-bone tender, and then with the risotto. The results are excellent. This risotto will amply serve 6 as an entrée.

CONDIMENTI	3 tablespoons unsalted butter
	1 rabbit, about 5 pounds, boned and cut into 1-inch pieces (you should have about 3 pounds of boned meat)
	2 garlic cloves, finely minced
	¼ cup chopped fresh parsley
	¼ teaspoon peperoncino (hot red pepper flakes)
	Salt and freshly ground white pepper
	¼ cup grated Pecorino Romano cheese
BRODO	10½ cups Basic Broth (see page 14), approximately
SOFFRITTO	6 tablespoons (approximately) pan drippings from sauté of rabbit
RISO	3 cups Arborio rice

1. CONDIMENTI: Preheat oven to 350°F. Heat the butter in a heavy 6- to 8-quart casserole over moderate heat. When it begins to foam, add the rabbit and sauté for about 5 minutes, while stirring, until all the pieces are well browned. Transfer the rabbit to another heavy 3- to 4-quart casserole and add the garlic, parsley, peperoncino, salt and pepper to taste, and enough broth to cover, about 1½ cups. Cover the casserole and put in the preheated oven. Cook for 1 hour. Reserve the pan juices from sautéing the rabbit in the first casserole and use as the soffritto for the risotto.

2. BRODO: Bring the broth to a steady simmer in a saucepan on top of the stove.

3. SOFFRITTO: Heat the pan drippings from sautéing the rabbit.

4. RISO: Add the rice to the soffritto; using a wooden spoon, stir

for 1 minute, making sure all the grains are well coated. Add the rabbit meat and cooking juices and stir until the juices are completely absorbed. Begin to add the simmering broth, ½ cup at a time, stirring frequently. Wait until each addition is almost completely absorbed before adding the next ½ cup, reserving about ¼ cup to add at the end. Stir frequently to prevent sticking.

5. After approximately 18 minutes, when the rice is tender but still firm, add the reserved broth. Turn off the heat and add the remaining condimenti—Romano cheese—and stir vigorously to combine with the rice. Serve immediately.

Serves 8

Rabbit, Herbs, and Vegetables

RISOTTO
PALIO

Andrea Hellrigl created this risotto especially for Palio—a grand restaurant that offers the best of the *nuova cucina* in New York City. The recipe calls for rabbit broth, but Basic Meat Broth (see page 13) can be substituted.

CONDIMENTI	1 small rabbit (approximately 3 pounds)
	½ cup virgin olive oil
	1 teaspoon finely minced garlic
	1 teaspoon finely chopped fresh rosemary
	1 cup dry white wine
	½ cup rabbit broth or Basic Meat Broth (see page 13)
	Salt and freshly ground black pepper
	4 tablespoons finely diced blanched carrot
	4 tablespoons fresh shelled peas or defrosted frozen peas, not cooked
	4 tablespoons chopped fresh tomatoes that have been peeled and seeded
	4 tablespoons finely diced zucchini
	4 or 5 basil leaves, cut julienne
	4 tablespoons unsalted butter
	4 tablespoons grated Parmesan cheese
SOFFRITTO	2 tablespoons unsalted butter
	1 teaspoon finely minced shallots
RISO	1½ cups Arborio rice
BRODO	5 cups Rabbit Broth or Basic Meat Broth (see page 13), approximately

1. CONDIMENTI: Preheat oven to 450°F. Bone the rabbit and clean away the hard skin. (You should have ¾ to 1 pound of rabbit meat.) Cut into small dice. Marinate the rabbit with ¼ cup of the olive oil, minced garlic, and rosemary for about 2 to 3 hours. Make a strong broth with rabbit bones and scraps (omit this if you are using prepared meat broth). Heat a small roasting pan and add the rabbit and the marinade. Place in the hot oven and roast to a golden brown; do not allow the meat to get too brown. Add the white wine and rabbit broth (or meat broth) and continue roasting until the liquids are reduced by about three-quarters and the meat is very tender.

2. In a skillet, heat the remaining ¼ cup olive oil and add the diced vegetables. Sauté quickly for about 2 to 3 minutes, season with salt and pepper, and add the basil. Set aside.

3. *SOFFRITTO:* Heat the butter in a heavy 4-quart casserole over moderate heat. Add the shallots and sauté until they begin to soften, for about 1 to 2 minutes, being careful not to brown them.

4. *RISO:* Add the rice and, using a wooden spoon, stir for 1 minute, making sure all the grains are well coated. Begin to add the simmering broth ½ cup at a time, stirring frequently. Wait until each addition is almost completely absorbed before adding the next ½ cup. Stir frequently to prevent sticking.

5. After approximately 18 minutes, when the rice is tender but still firm, add the diced rabbit and the vegetables. Turn off the heat and add the remaining condimenti—butter and Parmesan—and stir to combine with the rice. Serve immediately.

Serves 4

Fennel Sausage

RISOTTO
ALLA TOSCANA

Throughout Tuscany you can find many variations of risotto with sausage. This one calls for mildly cured, fennel-flavored sausage. Although the taste is slightly different from the Tuscan variety, a good substitute is fresh fennel sausage, which we find widely sold in supermarkets and Italian food shops. Remove the casing from the sausage before you cook it, then sauté with the onion and butter mixture.

BRODO	5½ cups Basic Broth (see page 14), approximately

SOFFRITTO	2 tablespoons unsalted butter
	1 tablespoon oil
	⅓ cup finely minced onion
	2 tablespoons finely minced carrot
	2 tablespoons finely minced celery

CONDIMENTI	3 ounces fresh fennel sausage, or 1 average-size sausage, casing removed
	1 tablespoon unsalted butter
	⅓ cup grated Parmesan cheese
	1 tablespoon finely chopped fresh parsley
RISO	1½ cups Arborio rice

1. BRODO: Bring the broth to a steady simmer in a saucepan on top of the stove.

2. SOFFRITTO: Heat the butter and oil in a heavy 4-quart casserole over moderate heat. Add the onion, carrot, and celery and sauté for 1 to 2 minutes, until the onion begins to soften, being careful not to brown it.

3. CONDIMENTI: Add the sausage to the soffritto; using a fork, break up the meat and stir until it loses its pink color and begins to brown.

4. RISO: Add the rice; using a wooden spoon, stir for 1 minute, making sure all the grains are well coated. Begin to add the simmering broth, ½ cup at a time, stirring frequently. Wait until each addition is almost completely absorbed before adding the next ½ cup, reserving about ¼ cup to add at the end. Stir frequently to prevent sticking.

5. After approximately 18 minutes, when the rice is tender but still firm, add the reserved broth. Turn off the heat and immediately add the remaining condimenti—butter, Parmesan, and parsley—and stir vigorously to combine with the rice. Serve immediately.

Serves 4

Sausage, Artichoke, & Peas

RISOTTO
ALLA GENOVESE

The sausage gives a hearty flavor to this risotto of sliced fresh artichokes and sweet tender peas, while the mozzarella lends just the right amount of creaminess. Serve as a second course preceded by a simple salad of grated carrots on a bed of lettuce greens in a tangy vinaigrette dressing.

CONDIMENTI	3 ounces Italian sausage meat, or 1 average-size sausage, casing removed
	1 medium-size artichoke, trimmed, choke removed, and sliced (see recipe for Risotto con i Carciofi, page 79)
	½ cup fresh peas or defrosted frozen baby peas, not cooked
	½ cup shredded mozzarella cheese
	¼ cup grated Parmesan cheese
BRODO	6 cups Basic Broth (see page 14), approximately
SOFFRITTO	2 tablespoons unsalted butter
	1 tablespoon oil
	⅓ cup finely minced onion
	2 tablespoons minced carrot
	2 tablespoons minced celery
RISO	1½ cups Arborio rice

1. CONDIMENTI: Place the sausage in a skillet over moderate heat. Using a fork, break up the meat and cook until it loses its pink color and begins to brown. Add the sliced artichoke and stir to combine it with the meat. Pour in 1 cup of basic broth. Cover the pan, turn the heat to moderate-low, and allow the meat and artichoke mixture to simmer for 20 minutes while you prepare the risotto.

2. BRODO: Bring remaining broth to a steady simmer in a saucepan on top of the stove.

3. SOFFRITTO: Heat the butter and oil in a heavy 4-quart casserole over moderate heat. Add the onion, carrot, and celery and sauté for 1 to 2 minutes, until the onion begins to soften, being careful not to brown it.

4. RISO: Add the rice to the soffritto; using a wooden spoon, stir for 1 minute, making sure all the grains are well coated. Begin to add the simmering broth, ½ cup at a time, stirring frequently. Wait until each addition is almost completely absorbed before adding the next ½ cup, reserving about ¼ cup to add at the end. Stir frequently to prevent sticking.

5. After approximately 18 minutes, when the rice is tender but still firm, add the reserved broth and the condimenti—the sausage and artichoke mixture, peas, mozzarella, and Parmesan—and stir until the cheeses are melted and combined with the rice. Serve immediately.

Serves 4

Sweet & Hot Sausages

RISOTTO PICCANTE

The hot sausage and red pepper make this a delicious one-alarm risotto. You can always increase the amount of hot pepper flakes for an even more fiery effect. Serve this with some good crusty bread.

BRODO	5 cups Basic Broth (see page 14), approximately
	½ cup dry white wine or broth
SOFFRITTO	2 tablespoons unsalted butter
	1 tablespoon olive oil
	⅓ cup finely minced onion
RISO	1½ cups Arborio rice
CONDIMENTI	3 ounces sweet sausage meat, or 1 average-size sausage, casing removed
	3 ounces hot sausage meat, or 1 average-size sausage, casing removed
	1 tablespoon unsalted butter
	½ teaspoon peperoncino (hot red pepper flakes)
	⅓ cup grated Parmesan cheese
	1 tablespoon finely chopped fresh parsley

1. BRODO: Bring the broth to a steady simmer in a saucepan on top of the stove.

2. SOFFRITTO: Heat the butter and oil in a heavy 4-quart casserole over moderate heat. Add the onion and sauté for 1 to 2 minutes, until it begins to soften, being careful not to brown it.

3. RISO: Add the rice to the soffritto; using a wooden spoon, stir for 1 minute, making sure all the grains are well coated. Add the wine and stir until it is completely absorbed.

4. CONDIMENTI: Add the sausage to the rice; using a fork, stir until the meat loses its pink color. Begin to add the simmering broth, ½ cup at a time, stirring frequently. Wait until each addition is almost completely absorbed before adding the next ½ cup, reserving about ¼ cup to add at the end. Stir frequently to prevent sticking.

5. After approximately 18 minutes, when the rice is tender but still firm, add the reserved broth. Turn off the heat and immediately add the remaining condimenti—butter, peperoncino, Parmesan, and parsley—and stir vigorously to combine with the rice. Serve immediately.

Serves 4

VARIATIONS

1. Add a pinch of powdered saffron to the rice with the first addition of broth in step 4.

2. Add ½ cup fresh peas or defrosted frozen peas, not cooked, in step 5 with the condimenti.

Sausage & Pecorino Cheese

RISOTTO
ALLA SARDA

"Pecorino" is the general name for all of the Italian cheeses made with sheep's milk. This risotto gets its character from the distinctive sharp flavor of the cheese known as "Pecorino Romano," which is produced in Sardinia and Sicily. Serve this risotto with a red wine, such as Bardolino or Valpolicella.

CONDIMENTI	2 tablespoons chopped pancetta or blanched salt pork
	3 ounces fresh sausage meat, or 1 Italian sausage, casing removed
	2 small tomatoes, peeled, seeded, and chopped, or ½ cup canned Italian tomatoes, well drained and chopped
	Pinch of powdered saffron
	1 tablespoon unsalted butter
	⅓ cup grated Pecorino Romano cheese
	1 tablespoon finely chopped fresh parsley
BRODO	5½ cups Basic Broth (see page 14), approximately

SOFFRITTO	2 tablespoons unsalted butter
	1 tablespoon oil
	⅓ cup finely minced onion

RISO	1½ cups Arborio rice

1. CONDIMENTI: Place the pancetta in a small skillet over moderate heat and cook for 3 to 5 minutes, until it begins to render its fat. Add the sausage meat; using a fork, break it up while stirring until it loses its pink color and begins to brown. Add the tomatoes and saffron, lower the heat to simmer, and cook the meat and tomatoes for 20 minutes while the risotto is being prepared. Stir occasionally.

2. BRODO: Bring the broth to a steady simmer in a saucepan on top of the stove.

3. SOFFRITTO: Heat the butter and oil in a heavy 4-quart casserole over moderate heat. Add the onion and sauté for 1 to 2 minutes, until it begins to soften, being careful not to brown it.

4. RISO: Add the rice to the soffritto; using a wooden spoon, stir for 1 minute, making sure all the grains are well coated. Begin to add the simmering broth, ½ cup at a time, stirring frequently. Wait until each addition is almost completely absorbed before adding the next ½ cup, reserving about ¼ cup to add at the end. Stir frequently to prevent sticking.

5. After approximately 18 minutes, when the rice is tender but still firm, add the reserved broth. Turn off the heat and add the condimenti—the sausage and tomato mixture, butter, Romano, and parsley—and stir vigorously to combine with the rice. Serve immediately.

Serves 4

NOTE: You may substitute Asiago, another flavorful hard grating cheese. While Parmesan can be used in this recipe, it will not give the pungent flavor of Pecorino.

Sausage, Mushrooms, Lettuce, & Raisins

RISOTTO
ALLA GRECA

This risotto is more akin to Greece than Italy. After tasting the hearty, savory flavor of the sausage and mushrooms with the slightly sweet raisins, we were captivated by this exotic dish.

CONDIMENTI	6 ounces Italian sausage, or 2 average-size sausages, casings removed
	2 garlic cloves, finely minced
	4 ounces white mushrooms, cleaned, stems removed, and sliced (about 1 cup)
	½ head of Boston or Romaine lettuce, washed, dried, spines cut away, and finely shredded (1 cup)
	1½ ounces raisins (about ⅓ cup)
	⅓ cup grated Parmesan cheese
BRODO	5½ cups Basic Broth (see page 14), approximately
	½ cup dry white wine or broth

SOFFRITTO	2 tablespoons unsalted butter
	1 tablespoon oil
	3 tablespoons finely minced onion
	2 tablespoons minced carrot
	2 tablespoons minced celery

RISO	1½ cups Arborio rice

1. CONDIMENTI: Place the sausage meat with the garlic in a skillet over moderate heat. Using a fork, break up the meat and cook, while stirring, until the meat loses its pink color and begins to brown. Turn the heat to moderate-low and add the mushrooms, lettuce, and raisins, and continue to cook for 10 minutes. Turn off the heat and set aside.

2. BRODO: Bring the broth to a steady simmer in a saucepan on top of the stove.

3. SOFFRITTO: Heat the butter and oil in a heavy 4-quart casserole over moderate heat. Add the onion, carrot, and celery and sauté for 1 to 2 minutes, until the onion begins to soften, being careful not to brown it.

4. RISO: Add the rice to the soffritto; using a wooden spoon, stir for 1 minute, making sure all the grains are well coated. Add the wine and stir until it is completely absorbed. Begin to add the simmering broth, ½ cup at a time, stirring frequently. Wait until each addition is almost completely absorbed before adding the next ½ cup, reserving about ¼ cup to add at the end. Stir frequently to prevent sticking.

5. After approximately 18 minutes, when the rice is tender but still firm, add the reserved broth and the condimenti—the sausage-mushroom-lettuce-raisin mixture and the Parmesan—and stir vigorously to combine with the rice. Serve immediately.

Serves 4

Prosciutto

RISOTTO
AL PROSCIUTTO

Although you can use any prosciutto in this risotto, nothing quite compares to the genuine article, imported Italian prosciutto, with its incredibly mild, almost sweet, and only slightly salty taste. The added cream makes this risotto surprisingly light.

BRODO	5 cups Basic Broth (see page 14), approximately
	½ cup dry white wine
SOFFRITTO	2 tablespoons unsalted butter
	1 tablespoon oil
	⅓ cup finely minced onion
RISO	1½ cups Arborio rice
CONDIMENTI	3 to 4 ounces prosciutto, finely minced (about ½ cup)
	¼ cup light cream
	⅓ cup grated Parmesan cheese
	1 tablespoon finely chopped fresh parsley

1. BRODO: Bring the broth to a steady simmer in a saucepan on top of the stove.
2. SOFFRITTO: Heat the butter and oil in a heavy 4-quart casse-

role over moderate heat. Add the onion and sauté for 1 to 2 minutes, until it begins to soften, being careful not to brown it.

3. *RISO:* Add the rice to soffritto; using a wooden spoon, stir for 1 minute, making sure all the grains are well coated. Add the wine and stir until it is completely absorbed. Begin to add the simmering broth, ½ cup at a time, stirring frequently to prevent sticking. Wait until each addition is almost completely absorbed before adding the next ½ cup, reserving about ¼ cup for the very end. Stir frequently.

4. *CONDIMENTI:* After approximately 18 minutes, when the rice is tender but still firm, add the reserved broth and the condimenti—prosciutto, cream, Parmesan, and parsley—and stir vigorously to combine with the rice. Serve immediately.

Serves 4

VARIATIONS

1. Substitute diced lightly smoked country-style ham for the prosciutto.

2. For a new twist on a familiar first course, prepare risotto with prosciutto and melon. The sweetness of the melon contrasts with the saltiness of the ham and makes for an interesting taste sensation. Add about ⅓ cup finely diced cantaloupe in step 4, when you add the prosciutto and cream.

Prosciutto, Chicory, & Fontina

RISOTTO
AL PROSCIUTTO E CICORIA

This risotto with prosciutto, green-leaf chicory, and Fontina cheese is a satisfying meal in itself when accompanied by some good crusty bread and a full-bodied red wine, such as a Gattinara.

BRODO	5 cups Basic Broth (see page 14), approximately
	½ cup dry white wine or broth
SOFFRITTO	2 tablespoons unsalted butter
	1 tablespoon oil
	⅓ cup finely minced onion
	2 tablespoons finely minced carrot
	2 tablespoons finely minced celery
RISO	1½ cups Arborio rice
CONDIMENTI	3 to 4 ounces prosciutto, coarsely chopped (about ½ cup)
	1 cup chopped green chicory
	2 ounces Italian Fontina cheese, rind removed, cut into 1-inch pieces
	¼ cup light cream
	⅓ cup grated Parmesan cheese

1. *BRODO:* Bring the broth to a steady simmer in a saucepan on top of the stove.

2. *SOFFRITTO:* Heat the butter and oil in a heavy 4-quart casserole over moderate heat. Add the onion, carrot, and celery and sauté for 1 to 2 minutes, until the onion begins to soften, being careful not to brown it.

3. *RISO:* Add the rice to the soffritto; using a wooden spoon, stir for 1 minute, making sure all the grains are well coated. Add the wine and stir until it is completely absorbed.

4. *CONDIMENTI:* Add the prosciutto and the chicory and begin to add the simmering broth, ½ cup at a time, stirring frequently. Wait until each addition is almost completely absorbed before adding the next ½ cup, reserving about ¼ cup to add at the end. Stir frequently to prevent sticking.

5. After approximately 18 minutes, when the rice is tender but still firm, add the reserved broth and the remaining condimenti—Fontina, cream, and Parmesan—and stir vigorously until the cheeses are melted and combined with the rice. Serve immediately.

Serves 4

Pancetta, Tomatoes, & Peas

RISOTTO
ALLA PANCETTA

Pancetta is the Italian version of bacon, but it is rolled rather than left in slabs, and salted, never smoked. Combined with tomatoes and peas, this risotto brings out the mild-cured pancetta flavor, and the results are delicious.

CONDIMENTI	3 to 4 ounces pancetta, diced (about ½ cup)
	1 tablespoon finely minced onion
	3 to 4 large plum tomatoes, peeled, seeded, and chopped, or 1 cup canned Italian tomatoes, well drained and chopped, with their juice
	½ cup fresh peas or defrosted frozen baby peas, not cooked
	¼ cup grated Parmesan cheese
BRODO	5 cups Basic Broth (see page 14), approximately
	½ cup dry white wine or broth
SOFFRITTO	2 tablespoons unsalted butter
	1 tablespoon rendered fat from the pancetta
	⅓ cup finely minced onion
RISO	1½ cups Arborio rice

1. CONDIMENTI: Put the pancetta in a skillet over moderate-low heat and cook, stirring frequently, for about 10 minutes, until the pancetta has turned golden brown and rendered most of its fat. There should be about 3 tablespoons of fat in the pan. Remove 1 tablespoon of the rendered fat and set aside. Add the onion and tomatoes to the pancetta and continue cooking for about 5 minutes longer. Turn off the heat and set aside.

2. BRODO: Bring the broth to a steady simmer in a saucepan on top of the stove.

3. SOFFRITTO: Heat the butter and tablespoon of pancetta fat in a heavy 4-quart casserole over moderate heat. Add the onion and sauté for 1 to 2 minutes, until it begins to soften, being careful not to brown it.

4. RISO: Add the rice to the soffritto; using a wooden spoon, stir for 1 minute, making sure all the grains are well coated. Add the wine and stir until it is completely absorbed. Begin to add the simmering broth, ½ cup at a time, stirring frequently. Wait until each addition is almost completely absorbed before adding the next ½ cup, reserving about ¼ cup to add at the end. Stir frequently to prevent sticking.

5. After approximately 18 minutes, when the rice is tender but still firm, add the reserved broth and the condimenti—the pancetta and tomato mixture, peas, and Parmesan—and stir vigorously to combine with the rice. Serve immediately.

Serves 4

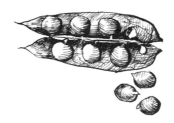

Pancetta, Eggs, & Cream

RISOTTO
ALLA CARBONARA

Borrowed from the pasta sauce, the combination of pancetta, eggs, and cream is every bit as delicious in risotto. If you cannot find pancetta, you can use salt pork or bacon (provided it doesn't have a strong hickory smoked flavor), but be sure first to blanch these substitutes for a minute or two in boiling water to remove some of their saltiness.

CONDIMENTI	2 ounces pancetta, diced (about ⅓ cup)
	½ cup light cream
	2 egg yolks, lightly beaten
	2 tablespoons grated Parmesan cheese
	Pinch of grated nutmeg
BRODO	5 cups Basic Broth (see page 14), approximately
	½ cup dry white wine or broth
SOFFRITTO	2 tablespoons unsalted butter
	1 tablespoon oil
	⅓ cup finely minced onion
RISO	1½ cups Arborio rice

1. CONDIMENTI: Place the pancetta in a skillet over moderate heat and cook, stirring frequently, until most of the fat has ben rendered and the pieces are well browned. Pour off all but 1 teaspoon of the fat (reserve it for another use or discard it), and return the pan to the heat. Pour in the cream and egg yolks; using a wire whisk, beat vigorously. Continue cooking for 2 to 3 minutes longer, until the cream and egg mixture has thickened slightly. Turn off the heat and set aside; cover to keep warm.

2. BRODO: Bring the broth to a steady simmer in a saucepan on top of the stove.

3. SOFFRITTO: Heat the butter and oil in a heavy 4-quart casserole over moderate heat. Add the onion and sauté for 1 to 2 minutes, until it begins to soften, being careful not to brown it.

4. RISO: Add the rice to the soffritto; using a wooden spoon, stir for 1 minute, making sure all the grains are well coated. Pour in the wine and stir until it is completely absorbed. Begin to add the simmering broth, ½ cup at a time, stirring frequently. Wait until each addition is almost completely absorbed before adding the next ½ cup, reserving about ¼ cup of broth to add at the end. Stir frequently to prevent sticking.

5. After approximately 18 minutes, when the rice is tender but still firm, add the reserved broth and the condimenti—the pancetta-cream-egg mixture, Parmesan, and nutmeg—and stir vigorously to combine with the rice. Serve immediately.

Serves 4

Salami

RISOTTO
AL SALAME

This risotto is a natural for salami lovers. In Italy it is typically prepared with a Milanese-type salami, made of ground pork and very little fat. We recommend using a Genoa salami because it has a mild flavor and is widely available. Serve with a salad of mixed greens and a light Chianti wine.

BRODO	5 cups Basic Broth (see page 14), approximately
	½ cup red wine, such as Montepulciano, Chianti Classico, or Brunello
SOFFRITTO	2 tablespoons unsalted butter
	1 tablespoon oil
	⅛ cup finely minced onion
RISO	1½ cups Arborio rice
CONDIMENTI	3 to 4 ounces Genoa salami, rind removed, very finely chopped (about ½ cup)
	1 tablespoon unsalted butter
	⅛ cup grated Parmesan cheese
	1 tablespoon finely chopped fresh parsley

1. BRODO: Bring the broth to a steady simmer in a saucepan on top of the stove.

2. SOFFRITTO: Heat the butter and oil in a heavy 4-quart casserole over moderate heat. Add the onion and sauté for 1 to 2 minutes, until it begins to soften, being careful not to brown it.

3. RISO: Add the rice to the soffritto; using a wooden spoon, stir for 1 minute, making sure all the grains are well coated. Add the wine and stir until it is completely absorbed. Begin to add the simmering broth, ½ cup at a time, stirring frequently. Wait until each addition is almost completely absorbed before adding the next ½ cup, reserving about ¼ cup to add at the end. Stir frequently to prevent sticking.

4. CONDIMENTI: After approximately 18 minutes, when the rice is tender but still firm, add the reserved broth and the condimenti—salami, butter, Parmesan, and parsley—and stir vigorously to combine with the rice. Serve immediately.

Serves 4

Liquor & Fruit Risotti

ITALY produces some of the finest wines in the world. Over the centuries many of these prized wines, with names such as Barolo, Amarone, Chianti, and Marsala, have earned a prominent place in the classic repertoire of risotto dishes. The key is to add the liquor or wine to the rice before any broth. This ensures that the alcohol sizzles away, leaving the rice with the flavor essence of the liquor.

On the other hand, with the exception of the risotto with grapes, which is a traditional recipe, fruit risotti are a relatively new invention. They have been created in recent years in the restaurants of Northern Italy by a few inventive chefs who were impressed with French *nouvelle cuisine*. Strawberries were the first to lend a subtle aura of fruit flavor to risotto. As more restaurants and cooks have embraced the *nuova cucina* (new Italian cooking), the list of fruit risotti has expanded to include apples, orange juice, grapefruit, and lemon.

Although the risotti made with fruit are the newest, most daring creations, while the liquor and wine risotti are among the oldest and most traditional recipes, both share a subtlety of flavor that gives the finished dish a unique, almost magical quality. The taste of the fruit or wine is at first only barely apparent to the palate, but with each mouthful the flavor emerges and becomes more deliciously pronounced.

White Wine

RISOTTO
AL VINO BIANCO

White wine is most often used in risotto as a flavor enhancer. In this risotto, white wine is the principal flavoring. Because so much of the taste of the wine comes through the risotto, we like to use a dry but full and fruity white wine, such as an Italian Chardonnay, Pinot Grigio, or Pinot Bianco. Add most of the wine when you begin to cook the risotto, saving a small amount to add toward the end of cooking. Serve this risotto as a first course or as an accompaniment to Lamb Stew (see Index).

BRODO	4 cups Basic Broth (see page 14), approximately
SOFFRITTO	2 tablespoons unsalted butter
	1 tablespoon oil
	2 tablespoons finely minced onion
RISO	1½ cups Arborio rice
CONDIMENTI	1¼ cups dry white wine
	1 tablespoon unsalted butter
	¼ cup grated Parmesan cheese
	1 tablespoon chopped fresh parsley

1. BRODO: Bring the broth to a steady simmer in a saucepan on top of the stove.

2. SOFFRITTO: Heat the butter and oil in a heavy 4-quart casserole over moderate heat. Add the onion and sauté for 1 to 2 minutes, until it begins to soften, being careful not to brown it.

3. RISO: Add the rice to the soffritto; using a wooden spoon, stir for 1 minute, making sure all the grains are well coated.

4. CONDIMENTI: Add 1 cup of the wine and stir until it is completely absorbed, reserving ¼ cup to add at the end. Begin to add the simmering broth, ½ cup at a time, stirring frequently. Wait until each addition is almost completely absorbed before adding the next ½ cup. Stir frequently to prevent sticking.

5. After approximately 18 minutes, when the rice is tender but still firm, add the remaining wine and stir well. Turn off the heat and immediately add the condimenti—butter, Parmesan, and parsley—and stir vigorously to combine with the rice. Serve immediately.

Serves 4

Chianti

═══════════

Chianti is among the few wines of the world that is made with a blend of red and white grapes, which gives it a distinctly light taste when compared to other red wines. It is a wine that we find particularly suited to risotto; it adds just enough flavor, but still allows the rich tastes of the butter and cheese to come through.

BRODO	4½ cups Basic Broth (see page 14), approximately
SOFFRITTO	2 tablespoons unsalted butter
	1 tablespoon oil
	2 tablespoons finely minced onion
	2 tablespoons finely minced carrot
	2 tablespoons finely minced celery
RISO	1½ cups Arborio rice
CONDIMENTI	1 cup Chianti Classico wine (see Note)
	1 tablespoon unsalted butter
	⅓ cup grated Parmesan cheese
	1 tablespoon chopped fresh parsley

1. BRODO: Bring the broth to a steady simmer in a saucepan on top of the stove.

2. SOFFRITTO: Heat the butter and oil in a heavy 4-quart casserole over moderate heat. Add the onion, carrot, and celery and sauté for 1 to 2 minutes, until the onion begins to soften, being careful not to brown it.

3. RISO: Add the rice to the soffritto; using a wooden spoon, stir for 1 minute, making sure all the grains are well coated.

4. CONDIMENTI: Add ¾ cup of the Chianti and stir until it is completely absorbed. Begin to add the simmering broth, ½ cup at a time, stirring frequently. Wait until each addition is almost completely absorbed before adding the next ½ cup. Stir frequently to prevent sticking.

5. After approximately 18 minutes, when the rice is tender but still firm, add the remaining ¼ cup Chianti and stir well. Turn off the heat and immediately add the remaining condimenti—butter, Parmesan, and parsley—and stir vigorously to combine with the rice. Serve immediately.

Serves 4

NOTE: Chianti has a long tradition of controversy in Italy. It is made with two varieties of red grapes, the Sangiovese and Canaiolo, and two white, Trebbiano and Malvasia. Government regulations call for 80 percent red grapes in the production of Chianti, a formula that was supposedly created in the nineteenth century. But producers, in an effort to make a better-tasting wine, have been known to alter the amount of white grapes, to reduce or even eliminate them altogether. While not all Italian Chianti is *Classico,* Chianti produced in a specific 430-square-mile zone in Tuscany that extends from just below Florence to Siena is considered to be the best. A few choice Chiantis are called *Riserva,* a term that Italian wine law applies to those wines that have had extra aging.

Marsala

RISOTTO
AL MARSALA

Marsala, the slightly sweet apéritif from Sicily, was created during the seventeenth century when great amounts of Sicilian wine were being shipped to England. For the rough trip on the open seas, the shippers would fortify the kegs with extra alcohol so that by the time the wine reached England, many months later, the flavor had intensified and the alcoholic content had soared. The results were so tasty that this process of fortification eventually became the process for making Marsala. This risotto has all the intense musky flavor and, depending on whether you use dry or sweet Marsala, some of the sweetness of the Marsala wine as well. We find that the sheep's milk flavor of Pecorino Romano cheese adds a nice contrast to the wine. Some mushrooms added to the soffritto make the dish even more flavorful.

BRODO	5 cups Basic Broth (see page 14), approximately
SOFFRITTO	2 tablespoons unsalted butter
	1 tablespoon oil
	¼ cup finely minced onion
	2 ounces white mushrooms, coarsely chopped (about ½ cup)
RISO	1½ cups Arborio rice

CONDIMENTI	¾ cup dry Marsala wine
	1 tablespoon unsalted butter
	¼ cup grated Pecorino Romano cheese
	1 tablespoon finely chopped fresh parsley

1. BRODO: Bring the broth to a steady simmer in a saucepan on top of the stove.

2. SOFFRITTO: Heat the butter and oil in a heavy 4-quart casserole over moderate heat. Add the onion and mushrooms and sauté for 1 to 2 minutes, until the onion begins to soften, being careful not to brown it.

3. RISO: Add the rice to the soffritto; using a wooden spoon, stir for 1 minute, making sure all the grains are well coated.

4. CONDIMENTI: Add ½ cup of the Marsala and stir until it is completely absorbed. Begin to add the simmering broth, ½ cup at a time, stirring frequently. Wait until each addition is almost completely absorbed before adding the next ½ cup, reserving about ¼ cup to add at the end. When the rice has been cooking for about 10 minutes, add the remaining ¼ cup of Marsala and continue to add the broth. Stir frequently to prevent sticking.

5. After approximately 18 minutes, when the rice is tender but still firm, add the reserved broth. Turn off the heat and immediately add the remaining condimenti—butter, Romano, and parsley—and stir vigorously to combine with the rice. Serve immediately.

Serves 4

Amarone

RISOTTO
ALL'AMARONE

At a wonderful lunch at the restaurant Da Aimo e Nadia on the outskirts of Milan, we were presented with a bottle of 1977 Amarone wine by Aimo, the owner. Although we knew that he intended for us to drink the wine, we carried it home and prepared one of our favorite risotti, Risotto all'Amarone. Naturally, to make more of a good thing, we drank some of the wine with the risotto.

BRODO	4½ cup Basic Broth (see page 14), approximately
SOFFRITTO	2 tablespoons unsalted butter
	1 tablespoon oil
	2 tablespoons finely minced onion
RISO	1½ cups Arborio rice
CONDIMENTI	1¼ cups Amarone wine
	1 tablespoon unsalted butter
	¼ cup grated Parmesan cheese
	1 tablespoon chopped fresh parsley

1. BRODO: Bring the broth to a steady simmer in a saucepan on top of the stove.

2. SOFFRITTO: Heat the butter and oil in a heavy 4-quart casserole over moderate heat. Add the onion and sauté for 1 to 2 minutes,

until it begins to soften, being careful not to brown it.

3. RISO: Add the rice to the soffritto; using a wooden spoon, stir for 1 minute, making sure all the grains are well coated.

4. CONDIMENTI: Add 1 cup of Amarone and stir until it is completely absorbed. Begin to add the simmering broth, ½ cup at a time, stirring frequently. Wait until each addition is almost completely absorbed before adding the next ½ cup. Stir frequently to prevent sticking.

5. After approximately 18 minutes, when the rice is tender but still firm, add the last ¼ cup of wine. Turn off the heat and immediately add the remaining condimenti—butter, Parmesan, and parsley—and stir vigorously to combine with the rice. Serve immediately.

Serves 4

Champagne

RISOTTO
ALLO CHAMPAGNE

Champagne's universal appeal has made this risotto a familiar sight on Italian restaurant menus. Made with dry Champagne, not the slightly sweet sparkling wine, Asti Spumante, the subtle Champagne taste becomes more pronounced with every bite. Serve this elegant dish before a festive entrée, such as a whole poached salmon, and be sure to serve Champagne with dinner.

BRODO 4½ cups Basic Broth (see page 14), approximately

SOFFRITTO	3 tablespoons unsalted butter
	1 tablespoon finely minced onion
RISO	1½ cups Arborio rice
CONDIMENTI	1¼ cups Champagne (see Note)
	¼ cup light cream
	1 tablespoon chopped fresh parsley

1. BRODO: Bring the broth to a steady simmer in a saucepan on top of the stove.

2. SOFFRITTO: Heat the butter in a heavy 4-quart casserole over moderate heat. Add the onion and sauté for 1 to 2 minutes, until it begins to soften, being careful not to brown it.

3. RISO: Add the rice to the soffritto; using a wooden spoon, stir for 1 minute, making sure all the grains are well coated.

4. CONDIMENTI: Add 1 cup of Champagne, reserving ¼ cup to add at the end, and stir until it is completely absorbed. Begin to add the simmering broth, ½ cup at a time, stirring frequently. Wait until each addition is almost completely absorbed before adding the next ½ cup. Stir frequently to prevent sticking.

5. After approximately 18 minutes, when the rice is tender but still firm, add the remaining ¼ cup of Champagne, the cream, and parsley, and stir vigorously to combine with the rice. Serve immediately.

Serves 4

NOTE: When using Champagne in risotto, as with any other wine, the alcohol cooks away, leaving the essence or flavor of the wine. Therefore it is important to use a good-tasting Champagne when making this risotto. Asti Spumante is often incorrectly called "the Champagne of Italy" because it is bubbly due to natural carbonation. However, it is not made with the *méthode champenoise* and is only a marginally good-tasting wine.

We recommend using any good dry sparkling wine, such as Italian dry spumante, a French Blanc de Blancs, Spanish Frexinet, or an American dry Champagne, such as Chandon.

Rum

RISOTTO
AL RHUM

The light rum lends a surprising dimension to this flavorful dish. Serve this risotto before a hearty entrée of braised or roasted veal.

BRODO	4½ cups Basic Broth (see page 14), approximately
SOFFRITTO	2 tablespoons unsalted butter
	1 tablespoon oil
	2 tablespoons finely minced onion
	2 tablespoons finely minced carrot
	2 tablespoons finely minced celery
	2 tablespoons chopped pancetta

RISO	1½ cups Arborio rice

CONDIMENTI	1 cup light rum
	1 tablespoon unsalted butter
	⅓ cup grated Parmesan cheese
	1 tablespoon chopped fresh parsley

1. BRODO: Bring the broth to a steady simmer in a saucepan on top of the stove.

2. SOFFRITTO: Heat the butter and oil in a heavy 4-quart casserole over moderate heat. Add the onion, carrot, celery, and pancetta and sauté for 1 to 2 minutes, until the onion begins to soften, being careful not to brown it.

3. RISO: Add the rice to the soffritto; using a wooden spoon, stir for 1 minute, making sure all the grains are well coated.

4. CONDIMENTI: Add ¾ cup of rum and stir until it is completely absorbed. Begin to add the simmering broth, ½ cup at a time, stirring frequently. Wait until each addition is almost completely absorbed before adding the next ½ cup. Stir frequently to prevent sticking.

5. After approximately 18 minutes, when the rice is tender but still firm, add the remaining rum and stir well. Turn off the heat and immediately add the remaining condimenti—butter, Parmesan, and parsley—and stir vigorously to combine with the rice. Serve immediately.

Serves 4

VARIATIONS

1. Add 3 ounces fresh Italian sweet sausage, about 1 sausage, casing removed, to the soffritto and continue with the directions.

2. Brandy or dark rum can be substituted for the light rum. Add it to the soffritto before you add the rice. It imparts a deep brown tone and enriches the flavor of the risotto.

Fruit Risotti

Orange Juice, Capers, Brandy

RISOTTO
ALL'ARANCIA

The intense flavors of the orange juice, capers, and brandy mellow when simmered with rice. This risotto calls for dark-fleshed blood oranges that are grown in Sicily and are used for eating, drinking, and cooking throughout Italy. They are now occasionally available in this country and should be used in this risotto if possible. Otherwise use freshly squeezed juice (juice made from concentrate won't give the right flavor) from our native oranges.

BRODO	4½ cups Basic Broth (see page 14), approximately

SOFFRITTO	2 tablespoons unsalted butter
	1 tablespoon oil
	⅓ cup finely minced onion
	1 tablespoon minced capers

RISO	1½ cups Arborio rice

CONDIMENTI	1 cup freshly squeezed orange juice, at room temperature
	2 tablespoons brandy
	2 tablespoons light cream
	¼ cup grated Parmesan cheese

1. BRODO: Bring the broth to a steady simmer in a saucepan on top of the stove.

2. SOFFRITTO: Heat the butter and oil in a heavy 4-quart casserole over moderate heat. Add the onion and capers and sauté for 1 to 2 minutes, until the onion begins to soften, being careful not to brown it.

3. RISO: Add the rice to the soffritto; using a wooden spoon, stir for 1 minute, making sure all the grains are well coated.

4. CONDIMENTI: Add the orange juice and stir until it is completely absorbed. Begin to add the simmering broth, ½ cup at a time, stirring frequently. Wait until each addition is almost completely absorbed before adding the next ½ cup, reserving about ¼ cup to add at the end. Stir frequently to prevent sticking.

5. After approximately 18 minutes, when the rice is tender but still firm, add the reserved broth and the remaining condimenti—brandy, cream, and Parmesan—and stir vigorously to combine with the rice. Serve immediately.

Serves 4

Lemon

RISOTTO AL LIMONE

The tart taste of the lemon juice and tender sweet peas makes this a refreshing first course. This is an excellent risotto to use for making croquettes (see page 314). Serve an entrée of grilled fish or chicken.

BRODO	5 cups Basic Broth (see page 14), approximately
SOFFRITTO	2 tablespoons unsalted butter
	1 tablespoon oil
	¼ cup finely minced onion
RISO	1½ cups Arborio rice
CONDIMENTI	½ cup freshly squeezed lemon juice, about 2 lemons
	¼ cup brandy
	1 cup fresh peas or defrosted frozen peas, not cooked
	¼ cup light cream
	⅓ cup grated Parmesan cheese

1. BRODO: Bring the broth to a steady simmer in a saucepan on top of the stove.

2. SOFFRITTO: Heat the butter and oil in a heavy 4-quart casse-

role over moderate heat. Add the onion and sauté for 1 to 2 minutes, until it begins to soften, being careful not to brown it.

3. RISO: Add the rice to the soffritto; using a wooden spoon, stir for 1 minute, making sure all the grains are well coated.

4. CONDIMENTI: Add the lemon juice and the brandy and stir until they are completely absorbed. Begin to add the simmering broth, ½ cup at a time, stirring frequently. Wait until each addition is almost completely absorbed before adding the next ½ cup, reserving about ¼ cup to add at the end. Stir frequently to prevent sticking.

5. After approximately 18 minutes, when the rice is tender but still firm, add the reserved broth and the remaining condimenti—peas, cream, and Parmesan—and stir vigorously to combine with the rice. Serve immediately.

Serves 4

VARIATION

Omit the peas; add 2 tablespoons snipped fresh chives or chopped fresh dill.

Apples

RISOTTO
CON LE MELE

This savory risotto is the new creation of an adventurous chef in Trento. The apples become tender without turning too soft, and their sweetness is mild and not overpowering. For best results use Golden Delicious apples. Serve this risotto as a side dish with game or with fried calf's liver.

CONDIMENTI	2 tablespoons unsalted butter
	2 cups diced Golden Delicious apples that have been peeled and cored (about 1 apple)
	⅓ cup grated Parmesan cheese
	⅓ teaspoon grated nutmeg
BRODO	5 cups Basic Broth (see page 14), approximately
	½ cup dry white wine or broth
SOFFRITTO	2 tablespoons unsalted butter
	1 tablespoon oil
	3 tablespoons finely minced onion
RISO	1½ cups Arborio rice

1. CONDIMENTI: Heat the butter in a skillet over moderate heat. When it begins to foam, add the apples and cook, stirring occasionally, until the apples are tender, about 10 minutes. Turn off heat and set aside.

2. BRODO: Bring the broth to a steady simmer in a saucepan on top of the stove.

3. SOFFRITTO Heat the butter and oil in a heavy 4-quart casserole over moderate heat. Add the onion and sauté for 1 to 2 minutes, until it begins to soften, being careful not to brown it.

4. RISO: Add the rice to the soffritto; using a wooden spoon, stir for 1 minute, making sure all the grains are well coated. Add the wine and stir until it is completely absorbed. Begin to add the simmering broth, ½ cup at a time, stirring frequently. Wait until each addition is almost completely absorbed before adding the next ½ cup, reserving about ¼ cup to add at the end. Stir frequently to prevent sticking.

5. When the rice has been cooking for 10 minutes, add the sautéed apples. After approximately 18 minutes, when the rice is tender but still firm, add the reserved broth and the remaining condimenti—Parmesan cheese and nutmeg—and stir vigorously to combine with the rice. Serve immediately.

Serves 4

VARIATION

Add 1 tablespoon finely grated lemon zest to the sautéed apples in step 1.

Grapefruit

RISOTTO
AL POMPELMO

Grapefruit juice adds its distinctive citrusy flavor—sweet, tart, and bitter all at once—which makes this risotto the perfect first course before fish or game dishes. Top each serving with diced grapefruit sections.

BRODO	5 cups Basic Broth (see page 14), approximately
SOFFRITTO	2 tablespoons unsalted butter
	1 tablespoon oil
	1 small leek, white part only, washed and finely chopped (about ½ cup)
	3 tablespoons finely chopped celery
RISO	1½ cups Arborio rice
CONDIMENTI	1 cup grapefruit juice, warmed (the juice of 1 whole grapefruit, approximately)
	1 tablespoon unsalted butter
	¼ cup grated Parmesan cheese
	1 tablespoon chopped fresh parsley
	4 grapefruit sections, diced

1. BRODO: Bring the broth to a steady simmer in a saucepan on top of the stove.

2. SOFFRITTO: Heat the butter and oil in a heavy 4-quart casserole over moderate heat. Add the leek and celery and sauté for 1 to 2 minutes, until the leek begins to soften, being careful not to brown it.

3. RISO: Add the rice to the soffritto; using a wooden spoon, stir for 1 minute, making sure all the grains are well coated.

4. CONDIMENTI: Add the grapefruit juice and stir until it is completely absorbed. Begin to add the simmering broth, ½ cup at a time, stirring frequently. Wait until each addition is almost completely absorbed before adding the next ½ cup, reserving about ¼ cup to add at the end. Stir frequently to prevent sticking.

5. After approximately 18 minutes, when the rice is tender but still firm, add the reserved broth. Turn off the heat and immediately add the remaining condimenti—butter, Parmesan, and parsley—and stir vigorously to combine with the rice. Serve immediately. Garnish each serving with some diced grapefruit.

Serves 4

VARIATION

Add to the soffritto 2 tablespoons each of diced red and yellow sweet peppers.

Grapes

RISOTTO
CON L'UVA

Large sweet and juicy Malaga grapes are traditional for this risotto, but our own seedless red grapes are an excellent substitute. A lot of butter and Parmesan cheese transforms this into a savory risotto with a delicate grape flavor. This is the perfect beginning for a dinner of sautéed chicken in a delicate white-wine sauce.

BRODO	5½ cups Basic Broth (see page 14), approximately
SOFFRITTO	2 tablespoons unsalted butter
	1 tablespoon oil
	2 tablespoons finely minced onion
RISO	1½ cups Arborio rice
CONDIMENTI	½ cup red seedless grapes, cut into halves
	2 tablespoons unsalted butter
	½ cup grated Parmesan cheese
	2 tablespoons chopped fresh parsley

1. BRODO: Bring the broth to a steady simmer in a saucepan on top of the stove.

2. SOFFRITTO: Heat the butter and oil in a heavy 4-quart casserole over moderate heat. Add the onion and sauté for 1 to 2 minutes, until it begins to soften, being careful not to brown it.

3. RISO: Add the rice to the soffritto; using a wooden spoon, stir for 1 minute, making sure all the grains are well coated.

4. CONDIMENTI: Add the grapes and begin to add the simmering broth, ½ cup at a time, stirring frequently. Wait until each addition is almost completely absorbed before adding the next ½ cup, reserving about ¼ cup to add at the end. Stir frequently to prevent sticking.

5. After approximately 18 minutes, when the rice is tender but still firm, add the reserved broth. Turn off the heat and immediately add the remaining condimenti—butter, Parmesan, and parsley—and stir vigorously to combine with the rice. Serve immediately.

Serves 4

Making Use of
Leftover Risotto

ON most occasions when you prepare risotto every spoonful will be consumed right down to the last grain of rice. However, there will be times when you will have risotto left over. While you can try to reconstitute the risotto with hot broth and butter, this will always result in overcooked rice that only barely resembles risotto.

But that doesn't mean you have to throw your risotto leftovers away. There are two basic ways to prepare leftover risotto.

The first, and our favorite, is to turn leftover risotto into *supplì*, delicate breaded and fried croquettes that are crispy and tender all at once. They may be served as an hors d'oeuvre, a first course, an accompaniment to an entrée, or a main course, particularly for lunch or a light supper.

Supplì are really very simple to make: The leftover risotto is first shaped, then lightly dredged with flour, dipped into beaten egg, coated with bread crumbs, and finally deep-fried in hot oil.

For best results the rice should be cold, the oil should be at 375°F., and the *supplì* should be eaten freshly cooked and hot.

Risotto Supplì

For the basic risotto recipe made with 1½ cups of rice have:

1 cup unbleached white flour
2 eggs, beaten
2 cups plain, unseasoned bread crumbs
1 to 2 quarts vegetable oil for deep-frying

1. Heat oil in a deep-fryer or heavy saucepan until it reaches 375°F.

2. Place the flour, eggs, and bread crumbs in separate shallow dishes.

3. Scoop out 2 tablespoons of risotto and form into patties, balls, or logs. Be careful not to make the forms too thick, otherwise the outside will brown before the inside becomes hot.

4. Roll each *supplì* in flour, patting off the excess, then dip into the egg, and finally into the bread crumbs, making sure the shapes are completely coated before moving from one dish to another.

5. Fry the croquettes in the hot oil for about 3 minutes, or until golden brown. Remove from the oil and allow to drain on paper towels. Serve immediately.

Serves 6 to 8

Risotto al Salto

Risotto al Salto is a thin pancake of cooked risotto that has been spooned and smoothed into a hot pan, fried in butter, and served with a sprinkling of grated Parmesan cheese. It is the traditional (and by many standards, only) preparation for using leftover risotto. Originally created by Milanese restaurateurs as a way of using their leftover Risotto alla Milanese, it became the traditional dish for après-theater supper celebrations around La Scala.

While al Salto was born as an expedient to utilize risotto leftovers, it has been greatly refined along the way. Today, the best Milanese restaurants offer a delicate Risotto al Salto that is never made from leftovers. Each day at the Restaurant Savini in Milan, for example, the risotto for al Salto is prepared in the late morning and then left to cool and reach room temperature. By evening, the risotto has just the right consistency and temperature for preparing the al Salto servings for their dinner customers.

The name al Salto, which is Italian for "jump," "leap," or "with a bounce," comes from the way the cook supposedly performs the flipping of the pancake. An accomplished al Salto chef will flick his wrist, giving his black steel frypan a skillful jerk that tosses up the pancake into an about-face.

If the chefs in Milan have perfected their flipping technique, they have also perfected their pans after years of use. Even though we came home from Milan with two special al Salto frying pans, we have only been able to consistently accomplish this dish using a spatula and a pan with a nonstick surface, and we recommend that you do the same. The "jump" is far less important than the final results. A perfect Risotto al Salto should be as thin as an ordinary pancake (not thick like a croquette), light and crispy, sometimes even a little crunchy, and very buttery.

Preparing Risotto al Salto

Although Risotto al Salto is traditionally prepared only with the saffron-flavored Risotto alla Milanese, we have found that the procedure lends itself to almost any risotto, provided it is not filled with large pieces of meat or vegetables, which would make frying difficult.

Basically, there are two types of risotto that can be used for making a Risotto al Salto pancake:

The first is any leftover risotto. It must be at room temperature before you can make the pancakes. Cold risotto right from the refrigerator will crack and fall apart if you try to spoon and smooth it into a thin pancake shape. This risotto, which will usually have cheeses and other condimenti in it, benefits from a small amount of lightly beaten egg mixed into it, which binds the rice and makes frying a relatively simple task.

Second is the risotto you prepare especially for making al Salto. In this case, you partially cook the risotto for 12 to 15 minutes instead of the full 18 minutes, then allow it to reach room temperature. You do *not* add any condimenti, such as butter and cheese. This partially cooked, still crunchy risotto will finish cooking while it is frying.

The preparation of the pancake calls for these ingredients:

> 1 cup cooked or leftover risotto,
>   at room temperature
> 1 egg, lightly beaten (optional)
> 2 tablespoons unsalted butter
> Grated Parmesan cheese

1. Combine the risotto with the beaten egg if you are using it. Heat 1 tablespoon of the butter in a 6-inch omelet pan or skillet with a nonstick surface over moderate heat. When the butter begins to foam, add the risotto to the center of the pan; using a wooden spoon, quickly flatten the risotto so that it evenly covers the bottom of the pan.

2. Allow the risotto to cook undisturbed for 5 minutes. Then begin to check the underside by lifting the edge with a spatula. When the side that is facedown in the pan has turned very brown, in 5 to 10 minutes, and the pancake holds together when you try to lift it with a spatula, it is ready to be turned.

3. To turn the pancake, take the pan off the heat and place a plate facedown on top of the pan (a plate larger than the pan will protect your hand and arm from burns when you turn the pancake). Holding the plate in place with one hand and the pan by the handle with the other hand, turn the pan and plate upside down so that the plate is on the bottom and the pan is on top. The pancake will be on the plate. Return the pan to the stove over moderate heat and add the other tablespoon of butter. When it begins to foam, slide the pancake off the plate and into the pan. Cook for 5 to 10 minutes longer, until the other side is nicely browned.

4. Slide the pancake out of the pan and onto a plate. Serve immediately, with grated Parmesan cheese.

NOTE: To make al Salto for 4, use a large 10-inch omelet pan or skillet with sloped sides. Use 2 tablespoons unsalted butter for each side, 2 cups risotto, and 2 lightly beaten eggs. Cook as directed.

Index

About the Authors

JUDITH BARRETT, a free-lance reporter and food writer, has been covering the food scene in Boston since 1977. She is a founding member of the Women's Culinary Guild. Her work has appeared in a number of national publications and her articles have appeared regularly in the Boston *Globe* since 1980. She has also developed recipes for the Grand Diplôme cookbook series.

Barrett lives in Cambridge, Massachusetts, with her husband and two children.

NORMA WASSERMAN, who divides her time between her homes in Verona, Italy, and Cambridge, Massachusetts, is one of the undisputed leaders of the Boston culinary establishment. Her gourmet food shop Formaggio Kitchen is to Boston and Cambridge what Dean & Deluca and The Silver Palate are to New York City.

Wasserman is also an accomplished artist and has provided all the illustrations and the jacket painting for the *Risotto* cookbook. Her work has appeared on numerous covers, including *Time* magazine. She has taught drawing at Harvard University, and the most recent edition of *The Natural Way to Draw,* a Houghton Mifflin classic, has a cover drawing by Wasserman.